gennaro's

EASY ITALIAN

To my lovely Mother
and my sister Filomena

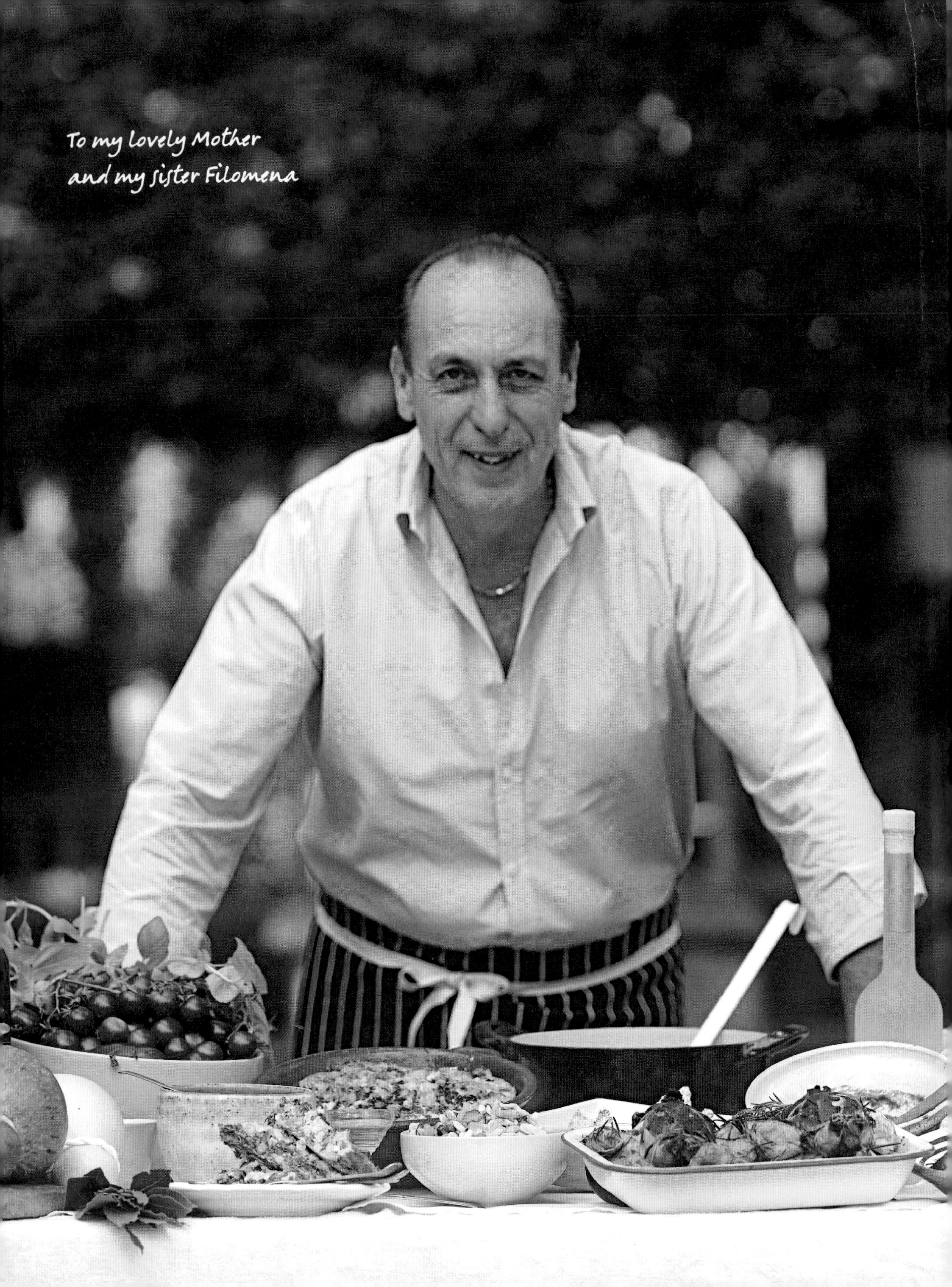

gennaro's
EASY ITALIAN

GENNARO CONTALDO

headline

First published in 2010 by
HEADLINE PUBLISHING GROUP

1

Cataloguing in Publication Data is available from the British Library

ISBN 978 0 7553 1788 2

Design and art direction by Nicky Barneby @ Barneby Ltd
Photography by Sam Stowell

Printed and bound in the UK by Butler Tanner & Dennis

Headline's policy is to use papers that are natural, renewable and recyclable products and made from wood grown in sustainable forests. The logging and manufacturing processes are expected to conform to the environmental regulations of the country of origin.

HEADLINE PUBLISHING GROUP
An Hachette Livre UK Company
338 Euston Road
London NW1 3BH

www.headline.co.uk
www.hachettelivre.co.uk
www.gennarocontaldo.com

Also by Gennaro:

Passione
Gennaro's Italian Year
Gennaro's Italian Home Cooking

Contents

Introduction

Simple, quick, seasonal – that's Italian food. No fuss, no complicated fancy patterns on the plate (well, how can you make a bowl of tagliatelle or spaghetti look pretty?), no complicated recipes, just good-quality, honest home cooking for everyday meals as well as more formal occasions.

My home cooking reflects what I do for restaurants – using different techniques to get the food to the customer on time, perhaps, but the recipes, the food and the simple honesty is the same throughout. I was once referred to as the 'honest' chef and I suppose it's true – in a cooking sense anyway! There aren't any gimmicks, my dishes are simple and straightforward – what you see is what you get. It is not served in a fancy way, but always tastes delicious and fresh. Once, I was asked to go to South Africa for the Cape Gourmet Festival and cook three separate menus during the week for food journalists, writers, chefs and basically the crème de la crème of foodie Cape Town. Months before my departure the details of my menus were required, along with photos showing my style of cooking. The South African organizers were most concerned when they saw my presentation – it was not what they had expected. They explained that they were looking for something more elaborate. But when I got there and they sampled the food in all its simplicity, they began to change their minds. Eventually, they agreed with me that Italian food was not about presentation but about subtle tastes and taste combinations. After that first successful year, I have been invited again and again.

Italy is changing and new tastes are being introduced through travel, foreign immigration and access to worldwide media. Italians are experimenting with exotic ingredients and restaurants serving non-Italian foods are opening in towns and cities there. It is quite strange for me to see when I return to Italy and it makes me a little sad but, at the same time, I am glad that Italians can finally taste dishes from far away, dishes which we in England have been taking for granted for many years. Young girls no longer sit for hours in their mother's kitchen watching them cook and writing down the recipes and techniques so they can recreate them in their marital homes. These days, young people are hunting the markets and shops for ginger, curry powder, lemongrass, yams and other such exotic delicacies. They then pass these new recipes on to their delighted friends and, sometimes, they even try – unsuccessfully – to pass them on to their mothers. Older generations of Italians reject this new type of cooking and are actually appalled by the look and combination of ingredients! But, however much they like to experiment with new tastes, young people still love their traditional Italian food. The exotic dishes are eaten as a treat and as something different, but they would never swap their daily plate of pasta for a curry. Not yet anyway!

When I was first asked to write this book, I argued that all the recipes in my books are easy – so how can we make this different? The point is, while these recipes aren't any simpler than the others, they are all quick to prepare and quick to cook. Sometimes you don't have the time to leave a succulent piece of meat roasting for hours – you are hungry and want a delicious, nutritious meal in no time at all. And that's what you'll find here. The recipes are still straightforward so even someone with only the most basic of cooking skills will be able to make them – but they are fast, too! Perfect everyday recipes for everyone.

Essential ingredients

When buying for your store cupboard, it is important to shop sensibly, as this will ultimately save you much time and money. And remember to stock up when something finishes.

Here is a list of my essentials and what I believe is needed for the perfect Italian kitchen.

Meat and dairy

Cooked ham

Pancetta – you can use bacon instead

Parma ham

Unsalted butter

Free-range eggs

Fontina – this has good melting properties, but can be replaced with cheddar

Mascarpone

Mozzarella – go for the hard variety sold in blocks. This is ideal for cooking and adding to salads. Buffalo mozzarella is best eaten very fresh as an antipasto

Parmesan – buy a whole chunk, not the ready-grated kind which is not the best quality and, quite frankly, you never know what odds and ends have been used to make it. Just grate what you need as you need it and wrap the remaining chunk in cling-film and store in the fridge

Ricotta

Fresh produce

Carrots

Celery

Chilli

Courgettes

Garlic

Herbs – a selection, e.g. parsley, rosemary, thyme, mint and basil

Leeks

Onions

Potatoes

Salad – a selection

Tomatoes

Frozen produce

Peas

Broad beans

Store cupboard

Anchovies

Baking powder

Black peppercorns

Breadcrumbs – ready-made

Candied peel

Capers

Chilli – dried and powdered

Chocolate

Cocoa powder

Couscous

Dried yeast

Flour – self-raising and plain, as well as semolina, polenta and potato flour

Gnocchi

Herbs – dried oregano, bay leaves and fennel seeds

Mixed dried fruit

Mixed nuts

Nutmeg

Oil – extra virgin olive oil and vegetable oil (for frying)

Olives

Pasta – a selection of short and long varieties

Plain biscuits – e.g. Rich Tea

Pulses and beans – a variety tinned and dried

Stock, powdered – chicken, beef, fish and vegetable

Rice – risotto (Arborio, Carnaroli or Vialone Nano) and long-grain

Salt

Sugar – caster and icing

Tomatoes – tinned and passata

Tuna

Vanilla – pods and essence

Vinegar – red wine, white wine and balsamic

Wine – red and white

Antipasti

I consider us lucky in Italy when it comes to antipasti or starters – they are so simple and speedy to prepare. The quickest and simplest of them all is the traditional platter of cured meats, such as prosciutto, speck, bresaola and salami, served with a few preserved vegetables and perhaps some fresh buffalo mozzarella. There is absolutely no cooking involved and you can be sure everyone will find a favourite to enjoy!

In Italy, antipasti are served on special occasions, such as Sundays, feast days like Christmas or Easter, or when friends are invited over. Most antipasto dishes can also be eaten as a light meal or snack.

Antipasto translated literally into English means 'before the meal', so when preparing this course, bear in mind that there will be at least one course after it, so make portions small and light. They should be yummy nibbles – just enough to stimulate the taste-buds for more delicious food to come.

I must admit, though, with all the wonderful antipasti that you can get, it is no wonder that Italians sometimes go over the top and bring out plate after plate of food. On a trip to Sicily once, we stayed in an agriturismo (a small rural hotel where all the produce is grown on the land) and after more than twelve hours of travelling, we had arrived just in time for dinner. For the antipasto course alone we were presented with ten dishes! There were aubergines, courgettes, peppers, tomato dishes, local cheese and salami, all with homemade bread and washed down with their own wine. Amazingly we carried on and two primo courses, two main courses, dessert and fruit later, we collapsed into bed! Strangely, we didn't feel overly bloated – I'm not sure if this was because we had not eaten properly all day or because the food was so natural, organic and untampered-with, it had made us feel good and healthy. On special occasions, such as a wedding, you can expect to find quite an array of antipasto dishes, some cold and some hot, rather like the ones we had in the agriturismo. The antipasti could also be themed – all the dishes could be based on fish and seafood, or a particular ingredient, depending upon the location and season.

Caprese nel bicchiere
Virgin Mary Italian-style!

400ml/14fl oz tomato juice

ice cubes (optional)

2 tablespoons extra virgin olive oil

a few drops of Tabasco sauce

2 cherry tomatoes, halved or quartered

2 mozzarella balls (bocconcini), halved or quartered

a few basil leaves, to garnish

salt and pepper

This is a very different way of serving the classic caprese salad (tomato and mozzarella). It's a great, refreshing starter packed with vitamins and hardly any calories. England meets Italy!

Pour the tomato juice into two glasses with the ice cubes. Divide the olive oil and Tabasco between them, and season with salt and pepper. Stir well.

Garnish with small skewers or toothpicks, alternating the tomato, mozzarella and basil. Serve immediately.

Verdure con crema di cipolle e rafano

Vegetables served with an onion and horseradish sauce

500g/1lb 2oz broccoli florets

90ml/6 tablespoons extra virgin olive oil

pinch of red chilli, finely chopped

1 garlic clove, squashed and left whole

350g/12oz escarole, cleaned and divided into 4–6 bunches

180g/6oz radicchio, sliced lengthways

salt and pepper

for the sauce

150g/5½oz red onion, cleaned weight, very finely sliced

200ml/7fl oz white wine

100ml/3½fl oz water

100ml/8 tablespoons extra virgin olive oil

2 teaspoons creamed horseradish

pinch of salt

This recipe seems complicated but it is really very simple to prepare. The vegetables need to be cooked separately but there is nothing difficult about it. Once they are cooked, prepare the simple sauce and serve. It is a perfect starter for when you have guests – the vegetables can be served on a big plate in the middle of the table and everyone can help themselves, dipping them into the sauce as they eat.

Cook the broccoli florets in boiling water for 2 minutes. Remove and drain, reserving a little of the cooking water. Heat two tablespoons of the olive oil in a pan over a medium heat, add the chilli and garlic and cook for a minute. Lower the heat, add the broccoli and a couple of tablespoons of the broccoli water and sauté for about 10 minutes, partially covered, until tender. Remove and discard the garlic clove.

Meanwhile, steam the escarole for about 5 minutes.

Place the radicchio in a bowl and toss with the remaining olive oil, and season with salt and pepper. Put a non-stick frying pan over a high heat and add the radicchio portion. Stir-fry for about 3–4 minutes until tender.

To make the sauce, place the onion in a saucepan with the wine, put on a high heat and bring to the boil. Reduce the heat to medium and cook for about 3 minutes. Remove a few slices of onion and set aside for garnish.

Add the water to the onions in the pan and continue to cook for a further couple of minutes until tender, but not mushy. Drain and place in a bowl together with the olive oil and salt and blend together. Stir in the horseradish.

Arrange the cooked vegetables on a serving dish and serve with the onion sauce.

Spiedini di anguria e mozzarella
Salad of skewered watermelon and mozzarella

500g/1lb 2oz watermelon, peeled and cut into approx. 24 cubes

24 small mozzarella balls (bocconcini)

150g/5½oz Parma ham, cut into 16 pieces and rolled

handful of basil leaves

250g/9oz mixed baby salad leaves

salt and freshly ground black pepper

for the marinade

4 tablespoons extra virgin olive oil

2 tablespoons balsamic vinegar

a few basil leaves, roughly torn

salt and freshly ground black pepper

8 skewers approx. 30cm/12in long

A simple refreshing starter ideal for warm sunny days. Serve with good bread and a cool glass of white wine. When watermelon is not available, you can use the orange-fleshed cantaloupe melon instead.

Place all the marinade ingredients in a bowl and mix well. Place the watermelon cubes and mozzarella balls in the marinade, and leave for 4 minutes.

Arrange the skewers with the watermelon, mozzarella and Parma ham pieces alternating with basil leaves. Set aside while you toss the salad leaves in the marinade – if necessary add more olive oil and balsamic vinegar – season with salt and pepper.

Place the salad in a serving dish and top with the skewers.

Caprino con composta di prugne
Grilled Caprino cheese with plums

500g/1lb 2oz plums, pitted and chopped

120g/4½oz sugar

1 tablespoon water

200g/7oz Caprino cheese (mild goat's cheese), sliced into 4 portions

some chives, finely chopped, to garnish

drizzle of balsamic vinegar (optional)

An easy and simple starter that looks most impressive. If you prefer, you can replace the Caprino with hard mozzarella.

Place the plums, sugar and water in a saucepan, and leave to gently simmer for about 20 minutes over a low heat until the plums turn soft and mushy.

Place the cheese on a hot flat griddle pan for about a minute until golden, then turn to colour the other side.

Remove from the pan and place on a plate with the plums alongside. Sprinkle with chives, drizzle with balsamic vinegar, if desired, and serve.

Melanzana in zucchine
Courgettes with an aubergine filling

2 large courgettes, approx. 150g/
5½oz each

4 tablespoons extra virgin olive oil,
plus extra for drizzling and
greasing

1 shallot, finely chopped

300g/10½oz aubergine, finely
chopped

a few rosemary needles

20g/¾oz Parmesan cheese, freshly
grated

a few thyme leaves

80g/3oz stale bread, crusts
removed and finely chopped

salt and freshly ground black
pepper

A lovely hot starter of hollow courgette shells stuffed with aubergine and herbs. The topping of finely chopped stale bread gives the dish a lovely crunchy texture. You could replace the aubergines with button mushrooms, if preferred.

Pre-heat the oven to 220°C/425°F/Gas 7.

Cut the courgettes in half and then again lengthways in half and scoop out and discard most of the white flesh. Cook the courgette shells in boiling water for about 4–5 minutes until tender but still firm.

Heat the olive oil in a frying pan and sweat the shallot. Add the aubergine and rosemary, season with salt and pepper, and stir-fry on a medium heat until the aubergines are soft.

Remove from the heat and add the Parmesan and thyme leaves. Fill the courgette shells with this mixture, top with the finely chopped stale bread, and drizzle with a little olive oil.

Place on a greased baking dish and bake in the oven for 20 minutes until golden.

Remove from the oven, leave to rest for a couple of minutes and then serve.

Tip: If you don't have any stale bread, use whatever you have at home.

Pizzette di melanzana fritte
Tomato and mozzarella on an aubergine crust

3 tomatoes, cubed

3 tablespoons extra virgin olive oil

handful of fresh basil, roughly chopped

400g/14oz aubergine

plain flour for dusting

3 eggs, beaten

25g/1oz Parmesan cheese, freshly grated

300g/10½oz breadcrumbs

oil for frying

300g/10½oz mozzarella, cubed

salt and pepper

This is another one of my variations of melanzana parmigiana. It is quicker and simpler to prepare and lighter to enjoy because of the fresh tomatoes, and makes an ideal starter or snack.

Pre-heat the oven to 200°C/400°F/Gas 6.

Combine the tomatoes, olive oil and half of the basil, season with salt and leave to marinate.

Top and tail the aubergines. Slice them into rounds ½cm/¼in thick and dust them with flour.

Combine the beaten eggs and Parmesan, and season with salt and pepper.

Dip the floured aubergine slices in the egg mixture and then in the breadcrumbs.

Heat abundant oil in a frying pan and fry the aubergines on both sides until golden. Remove and drain on kitchen paper.

Place the aubergine slices on a baking tray, top each one with some cubed mozzarella and place in the pre-heated oven for a few minutes. Once the mozzarella is just beginning to melt, remove from the oven, top with the marinated tomato and the remaining basil, and serve hot or cold.

Bruschette saporite
Roast tomato bruschetta with capers

400g/14oz cherry tomatoes

2 garlic cloves, finely chopped

30g/1oz capers

1 teaspoon oregano

90ml/6 tablespoons extra virgin olive oil

good-quality country bread, cut into 8 slices

salt

Instead of the usual topping of fresh raw tomatoes, for this bruschetta cherry tomatoes are roasted in the oven. The added ingredients of capers and garlic give the tomatoes more flavour, making this a very tasty starter. Remember to serve hot to enjoy the infusion of flavours at its best.

Pre-heat the oven to 200°C/400°F/Gas 6.

Place the tomatoes on a baking tray and sprinkle with the garlic, capers, oregano, salt to taste and drizzle with olive oil.

Roast in the hot oven for approximately 10 minutes until soft.

Meanwhile, toast the bread slices until golden. Arrange on a serving dish and top with the roast tomatoes. Serve immediately.

Scampi con insalata di agrumi
King prawns served with a salad of citrus fruit

12 king prawns (raw and in their shells), washed

1 bay leaf

50ml/2fl oz white wine

1 fennel, thinly sliced

1 honeydew melon (approx. 500g/1lb 2oz), cut into small cubes

1 pink grapefruit, peel and pith removed, thinly sliced into rounds

2 oranges, peel and pith removed, thinly sliced into rounds

green hairy bits from the fennel, to garnish

for the dressing

90ml/6 tablespoons extra virgin olive oil

juice of 1 orange

salt and pepper

A lovely refreshing starter that could even make a nice light lunch. It is delicate, nutritious and full of healthy precious vitamins. If you prefer, or are vegetarian, you could omit the prawns. Use blood red oranges when they are in season since they are sweeter and give a lovely pink colour to the salad dressing. Enjoy!

Place the king prawns in a saucepan with the bay leaf, wine and enough slightly salted water to cover the prawns. Bring to the boil and cook for 3 minutes. Remove and, when cool, peel and discard the shells.

To make the dressing, combine all the ingredients and mix well. Set aside.

Arrange the slices of fennel, melon, grapefruit and orange on either a large serving dish or divide between 4 individual plates. Place the king prawns around the edge of the plate/s, sprinkle with freshly ground black pepper and garnish with the fennel leaves.

Tip: Even if you use frozen prawns, they should be cooked as above.

Insalata di riso, melone e prosciutto
Rice salad with melon and Parma ham

200g/7oz long-grain rice

260g/9¼oz cantaloupe melon, cleaned weight and cubed

8 slices of Parma ham, roughly chopped

60g/2¼oz mozzarella, cut into small cubes

bunch of rocket

2 tablespoons extra virgin olive oil

salt and freshly ground black pepper

The classic Parma ham and melon has always been a popular starter in Italy and, even though it may not be thought of as trendy or original nowadays, I believe it is most people's favourite. As a slight variation, I have made it into a rice salad with the addition of mozzarella and rocket. The pungent taste of the rocket marries well with the sweetness of the melon and the saltiness of the Parma ham. Simple to make, try it for a starter or make more and serve it for a light summer lunch.

Cook the rice in plenty of slightly salted water according to the packet instructions. Drain and leave to cool.

When you are ready to eat, place the cooled rice in a large bowl and add the melon, Parma ham, mozzarella and rocket. Dress with the olive oil, season with salt and pepper and serve.

Tip: This recipe can be made in advance and stored in the fridge.

soups

Soups can be comforting, warming, seasonal, light, filling, nutritious and easy to make – there is no doubt that homemade soup makes you feel good.

Soup is very much a part of the Italian diet and is often eaten as the primo course instead of pasta or risotto. Soup can be light, like a simple broth with some pastina (small pasta shapes) added to it, or more substantial, like Minestrone (see page 43) with vegetables, beans and pasta. Soups can be seasonal – in spring I love making pea soup with peas fresh from their pods or a mixed herb soup with sorrel and nettles, which grow practically everywhere at that time of year. During autumn after a mushroom foray, I'll make a satisfying and delicious soup with all different kinds of wild fungi; in winter I go for root vegetable and rich bean soups, and in summer, cold soups such as cucumber or tomato can be very refreshing.

The variety of soups is endless and they can be made with just a few basic ingredients and some stock. You can whiz them smooth or enjoy all the chunky bits. They are quick and simple to prepare, can be made in advance, stored in the freezer or even kept hot in a thermos flask and taken as part of a packed lunch.

Remember – soup is easy to make, economical, a great first course if you've got a crowd round for dinner, and even a novice cook can make it!

Vellutata di broccoli e fave
Broccoli and broad bean soup

4 tablespoons extra virgin olive oil

3 slices pancetta or bacon, finely chopped

2 shallots, finely chopped

500g/1lb 2oz potatoes, roughly chopped

150g/5½oz fresh or frozen broad beans

200g/7oz broccoli, cut into florets

handful of fresh parsley, finely chopped, plus extra for garnishing

1.5 litres/2¾ pints hot vegetable stock

60g/2¼oz Parmesan cheese, freshly grated

salt and pepper

A healthy soup that uses only a few ingredients. Straightforward to prepare, it makes a nice change from serving broccoli as a side dish. I have used frozen broad beans for this recipe, but when they are in season, please do use fresh ones, if you prefer.

Heat the olive oil in a saucepan and sauté the pancetta or bacon and shallots. After a few minutes, add the vegetables and parsley, and stir well. Finally, pour in the stock and simmer for 35 minutes.

Remove from the heat and whiz in a blender until smooth. If the soup is a little too thick, add some more hot vegetable stock.

Stir in the Parmesan, season with salt and pepper, and place back on the stove over a low heat to warm through. Garnish with parsley leaves and serve immediately with toasted crostini, if desired.

Brodo di verdure
Vegetable broth

1 small onion

1 small courgette

1 carrot

1 celery stalk and leaves

1 potato

4 tablespoons extra virgin olive oil

1.5 litres/2¾ pints vegetable stock

This is a really quick way of making your own vegetable broth. I have used vegetable stock in the recipe to give the broth even more flavour but if your vegetables are home-grown and/or organic, you probably won't need to and can use water instead. Once you have the broth, you could add some small pasta shapes and serve as a soup, use it as stock to add to risottos, stews or other soups, or you can simply drink it as it is!

Peel all the vegetables and roughly chop into chunks. Place in a large saucepan with the olive oil and stock, and bring to the boil. Lower the heat to medium and simmer for 40 minutes.

Pass the broth through a fine sieve and use accordingly. You can return the vegetables to the broth to make a vegetable soup, or serve them separately, dressed with some extra virgin olive oil and a drop of wine vinegar.

Zuppa fredda di pomodori, carote e arance
Cold soup of tomato, carrot and orange

3 large oranges, peeled, deseeded and with the pith removed

4 ripe tomatoes, peeled and deseeded

2 celery stalks, finely chopped

3 carrots, peeled and grated

300ml/10fl oz tomato passata

1 tablespoon fresh basil or mint, finely chopped

extra virgin olive oil for drizzling

salt and pepper

Quick and simple to prepare, this is ideal served on a warm summer's day. Please make sure you use good-quality tomato passata – you could always make it yourself by blanching, peeling and deseeding vine tomatoes, then blending them to a smooth consistency.

Roughly chop the oranges in a bowl to ensure you preserve all the juice. Roughly chop the tomatoes. Place the oranges, orange juice, tomatoes, celery and carrots in a blender, and whiz until you obtain a creamy consistency.

Stir in the passata and basil or mint and season with salt and pepper to taste. Serve with a drizzle of olive oil.

Tip: To peel the tomatoes, place in hot water for a minute, drain and then the skin will come off easily.

Zuppa di patate e cipolle al forno
Credit crunch soup

700g/1lb 9oz floury potatoes, peeled and roughly chopped into bite-sized chunks

4 tablespoons extra virgin olive oil

300g/10½oz onions, finely chopped

1.2 litres/2 pints hot vegetable stock

pinch of chilli powder or freshly ground black pepper if you prefer

small bunch of chives, finely chopped

salt to taste

Not only is this soup economical, but it's a great standby if your cupboard is bare. It's cooked in the oven to give the potatoes and onions more flavour. You could liquidize the soup if you like, but I prefer it to have chunks. The addition of chilli powder really gives the soup a kick!

Pre-heat the oven to 200°C/400°F/Gas 6.

Parboil the potatoes in a saucepan of slightly salted water for 5 minutes. Drain well and set aside.

Drizzle 2 tablespoons of the olive oil into a deep-sided ovenproof dish. Add the potatoes, onions and half of the stock. Cover with foil and bake in the oven for 20 minutes until the potatoes are tender.

Remove from the oven and slightly mash about one third of the potatoes with a fork. Add the remaining stock, check for seasoning and, if necessary, add some salt. Mix well and place back in the oven uncovered for a further 15 minutes. If the soup starts to look dry, add more hot stock.

Remove from the oven, drizzle with the remaining olive oil, sprinkle with the chilli powder and chives, and serve immediately with toasted crostini, if desired.

Zuppa di pastanacchie, riso e prezzemolo
Parsnip, rice and parsley soup

4 tablespoons extra virgin olive oil

1 medium onion, finely chopped

350g/12oz parsnips, peeled and cubed

a few cherry tomatoes, quartered (optional)

200g/7oz Arborio rice

1.5 litres/2¾ pints hot chicken stock

handful of fresh parsley, finely chopped

salt and freshly ground black pepper

It is very popular to add rice to soups in Italy and very common to have Riso in Brodo, *which is simply broth with rice instead of the usual* pastina. *I love this type of soup when it is made with potatoes, but here I have replaced them with that lovely English root vegetable, parsnip, which gives the soup a very subtle sweet but pleasant taste. Serve this as soon as it is cooked, otherwise the rice will gradually absorb more of the liquid and you'll end up with a risotto-type consistency. It is also nice with grated Parmesan stirred in at the end.*

Pour the olive oil into a saucepan and sweat the onion over a medium heat for a few minutes. Next, add the parsnips and cherry tomatoes, if using, and sauté for a few more minutes.

Stir in the rice, making sure each grain is coated in the oil. Add the hot stock and simmer for about 15–20 minutes until the rice is *al dente* and the parsnips tender. Check the pan from time to time during cooking and if you notice the rice has absorbed a lot of the liquid, add more hot stock.

Once the rice is cooked, add more hot stock if you want a more liquid soup. Remove from the heat, season with salt and pepper, and stir in the parsley. Serve immediately.

Zuppa di pollo, porri e sedano
Chicken soup

1.2 litres/2 pints chicken stock

1 bay leaf

1 chicken breast, deboned, skinned and cut into small cubes

30g/1oz butter

2 tablespoons extra virgin olive oil

1 small onion, finely chopped

2 large leeks, finely chopped

2 celery stalks, finely chopped

1 tablespoon plain flour

few parsley leaves, to garnish (optional)

salt and freshly ground black pepper

The combination of chicken and leeks is lovely and this soup is so delicious that the only thing I can say is, make it! You won't be disappointed. I have suggested here that you blend the vegetables but, if you prefer, you can keep them whole.

Place the chicken stock and bay leaf in a saucepan and bring to the boil. Add the chicken breast, lower the heat and simmer for about 10–15 minutes until the chicken is cooked.

Discard the bay leaf, remove and set aside the chicken pieces, and reserve the stock.

In another saucepan, heat the butter and olive oil. Add the onions, leeks and celery, and sweat over a medium heat.

Meanwhile, place the flour in a bowl and gradually add half of the stock, stirring continually so as not to allow lumps to form. Stir this floured stock into the vegetable mixture. Add the remaining stock, bring to the boil and gently simmer for 15 minutes.

Remove from the heat and blend until you obtain a smooth consistency. Return to the heat, add the chicken pieces and gently warm through. Serve garnished with parsley and freshly ground black pepper, if desired.

Brodo di carne
Beef broth

800g/1lb 12oz strip loin beef, cut into chunks

approx. 1.8 litres/3 pints cold water

1 large onion, cut into quarters

1 large carrot, cut into chunks

2 celery stalks, cut into chunks, reserving some of the leaves

1 leek, cut into chunks

3 bay leaves

salt and pepper (optional)

For me this is the best broth in the world. It reminds me of home and childhood days as we waited for the broth to be cooked. It would be made with a large piece of beef and take hours to cook but, with the busy lives we all lead today, I have adapted the recipe so it can be cooked quickly, without losing any of the taste and nourishment of the original. In winter I often take the meat and vegetables out, once it has been cooked, to enjoy as a main course, reserving the liquid to have as a soup with small pasta shapes. You can, of course, use the liquid as a stock to add to risotto, or to make other soups or stews. The broth is also delicious on its own, drunk from a cup, to warm and soothe you on those dull cold winter days. The secret to this recipe is good-quality beef. I have suggested strip loin, which is a boneless sirloin, and this should be cut into medium-sized chunks, otherwise the cooking time has to increase.

Place the beef in a large saucepan with the cold water. Place on a high heat and bring to the boil. As it boils you will notice scum appearing on the surface: remove this with a slotted spoon.

Add all the vegetables, bay leaves, salt and pepper (if using), reduce the heat to medium and cook for 40 minutes. Cover with a lid, leaving a small gap for the steam to escape.

Switch off the heat, carefully remove the meat and large vegetables, and set aside. Pass the liquid through a fine sieve and use the broth accordingly.

Zuppa di lenticchie
Lentil soup

300g/10½oz brown or green lentils

1.8 litres/3 pints water

2 tablespoons extra virgin olive oil, plus extra for drizzling

2 garlic cloves, peeled and left whole

4 cherry tomatoes

4 small potatoes, peeled and chopped into small chunks

handful of fresh parsley, finely chopped

salt and freshly ground black pepper

A simple and delicate soup which is also very nutritious as lentils contain protein and are a great substitute for meat. If you want to make it more substantial, add some pasta and top with grated Parmesan.

Rinse the lentils in cold water and check for any impurities, although these days the bought varieties tend not to have any.

Place all the ingredients, except the salt and pepper, in a saucepan and bring to the boil. Once it is bubbling, reduce the heat to medium and cook for 30 minutes.

Remove from the heat and season with salt and pepper to taste. Drizzle with a little olive oil and serve with *crostone* if desired.

Tip: Crostone is a large slice of toasted, good-quality country bread and can be rubbed with garlic if desired.

Minestrone
Vegetable soup

75ml/5 tablespoons extra virgin olive oil

1 garlic clove, finely chopped

1 medium onion, finely chopped

1 celery stalk, finely chopped

1 tablespoon parsley, finely chopped

100g/3½oz spinach, roughly chopped

100g/3½oz Swiss chard, roughly chopped

100g/3½oz courgettes, sliced into rounds

1 large carrot, sliced into rounds

½ green cabbage, shredded

3 medium potatoes, peeled and roughly chopped

3 fresh plum tomatoes, peeled, deseeded and thinly sliced

1.5 litres/2¾ pints hot vegetable stock

100g/3½oz tinned borlotti beans, drained

200g/7oz fresh or frozen peas

200g/7oz short pasta, such as tubettini or shells

40g/1½oz Parmesan cheese, freshly grated

You get so many bad versions of this classic Italian soup – the worst are the tinned varieties – which is why I have included it in this book. Minestrone translated literally into English means Big Soup. It is a complete meal, made in one pot and is perfect for all the family. Although there are lots of ingredients involved, once all the chopping is done, it is so easy to make. If you don't like one of the vegetables, replace it with something else. And, if you prefer, use rice instead of pasta, or just make it with the vegetables. You could also serve it with a dollop of Pesto Sauce (see page 162).

Heat the olive oil in a large saucepan over a medium heat. Add the garlic, onion, celery and half of the parsley, and sweat for about 3 minutes.

Add the spinach, Swiss chard, courgettes, carrot and cabbage to the pan, stirring well. Next add the potatoes and tomatoes. Now, pour in the hot vegetable stock and simmer gently for 30 minutes.

Stir in the beans, add the peas and pasta, and continue to simmer until the pasta is *al dente*. Remove from the heat, sprinkle with the remaining parsley and the Parmesan. Leave to rest for a couple of minutes and then serve.

pasta

Pasta is probably one of the world's most popular and best-loved dishes – it certainly is for the Italians anyway! Most Italians eat pasta at least once a day, varying the shapes and sauces and, on special occasions like Sundays or feast days, making baked pasta dishes like cannelloni or lasagne.

Since living in England, I no longer eat pasta every single day but, even so, if I am in a country where good pasta is not easily available, then I really get a craving for it. I remember once when Liz and I were in Morocco, after days of wonderful Moroccan food, we were both really desperate for a simple plate of pasta. Luckily we met a Moroccan guy who used to live in Italy and was a great cook. That night, at our hotel, he prepared freshly made tagliatelle with tomato sauce – so simple but oh so delicious. Liz and I were in heaven!

Pasta is healthy, nutritious, inexpensive, and quick and simple to prepare. For me pasta is 'fast' food – quick to cook and the best sauces are uncomplicated and equally speedy to make. And, if you've made the sauce in advance, then it is even easier. It reminds me of when our girls were toddlers – quite often we would be returning home from a day out at about the time their dinner was due. Well, the screams could be heard for miles around. Liz would rush straight into the kitchen, put a pan of water on the heat to boil for the pasta, heat up some ready-prepared, homemade tomato sauce, grate some Parmesan, take off her coat and, hey presto, the girls' dinner was ready. Peace and quiet at last! It is still like that now, minus the screams, luckily.

Pasta is a meal in itself and doesn't require any fuss or lengthy preparation, and you can get a family meal on the table in just a few minutes. Nutritionally, pasta is also good – perfect for growing kids. It is an ideal carbohydrate because it releases energy slowly. It is highly digestible and the lack of fats makes it suitable for low-calorie diets, bearing in mind what goes into the sauce, of course.

There are so many different pasta shapes on the market. Apparently there are more than 600 different types available in Italy and, it is said, you could eat a different shape twice a day for a whole year! Well, I don't think I have tried that many, but there is certainly quite a selection to choose from these days, especially in Italy.

Italians insist that certain pasta shapes go with certain sauces and, to an extent this is true, but I believe it is something that only Italians truly understand. When my sister, Adriana, comes to stay, she and Liz are forever arguing about which pasta shape to use for a particular sauce. Liz, being only half-Italian and brought up in England, is happy to use any shape, but Adriana has to have the perfect one for the sauce.

Basically, long pasta, such as spaghetti or linguine, tends to go with quick-cook, light sauces, such as a simple tomato or fish sauce. Short shapes such as penne and fusilli marry well with heavier, more robust-tasting sauces, such as the popular arrabbiata sauce or the Roman amatriciana sauce.

When I visit my sister, Carmellina, in Italy, I am always amazed at how much pasta she keeps to hand. She dedicates a whole kitchen cupboard to it and when someone opens the cupboard, you have to watch your head, as packets tumble out! I don't expect anyone to keep such an array, but I do suggest you keep some long pasta, such as spaghetti, fusilli bucati and tagliatelle, and some short ones such as penne, farfalle and cavatelli, some lasagne sheets and some pastina (small pasta shapes).

For me, if there is not much in the cupboard, or if I'm in a hurry, or just tired and hungry, then pasta it is! Whichever shapes and sauces you prefer, I hope you will find my selection of recipes simple to prepare and, above all, delicious and enjoyable.

Spaghetti aglio, olio e peperoncino
Spaghetti with garlic, extra virgin olive oil and chilli

350g/12oz spaghetti

100ml/8 tablespoons extra virgin olive oil

4 garlic cloves, unpeeled and squashed

1 small red chilli, finely chopped – add more if you prefer a stronger flavour!

2 tablespoons parsley, finely chopped (optional)

I was almost reluctant to put this recipe in the book because of its sheer simplicity but, on second thoughts, the book is all about quick and simple dishes and this is such an Italian classic so I've kept it in! It is what Italians eat when there is nothing fresh in the fridge or they are so hungry they need to eat quickly. It is what young people cook after an evening out with friends – they all congregate in someone's kitchen in the middle of the night and make a spaghettata *with these few simple ingredients.*

Place a large saucepan of slightly salted water on the heat to boil and cook the pasta until *al dente*.

Meanwhile, in a large frying pan heat the olive oil, then add the garlic and chilli. Stir-fry for a couple of minutes on a high to medium heat, ensuring you do not burn. Remove the garlic and discard. Turn down the heat.

Drain the cooked spaghetti and place in the frying pan, mixing well so the spaghetti is coated with olive oil. Sprinkle with parsley, if using, and serve immediately.

Tip: If you like, you can add 4 anchovy fillets with the garlic and chilli for a more intense and salty flavour.

Penne alle verdure e ceci
Penne with vegetables and chickpeas

300g/10½oz penne

75ml/5 tablespoons extra virgin olive oil, plus extra for drizzling

1 medium onion, finely chopped

1 carrot, cubed

200g/7oz clean pumpkin, cubed

120g/4¼oz tinned chickpeas, drained

250ml/9fl oz hot vegetable stock

100g/3½oz Swiss chard, sliced into strips

needles of 1 rosemary branch, roughly chopped

salt and freshly ground black pepper

A quick and delicious pasta dish which is a meal in itself. Packed full of goodness, it is ideal for vegetarians. If you can't find Swiss chard you can use spinach.

Bring a large saucepan of slightly salted water to the boil, add the pasta and leave to cook until *al dente*.

Meanwhile, heat the olive oil in a saucepan and sweat the onion on a low heat for 2 minutes.

Add the carrot, pumpkin, chickpeas and half of the vegetable stock. Stir, cover with a lid and cook on a medium heat for 10 minutes. Add more stock if necessary.

Add the Swiss chard and half of the rosemary needles to the sauce. Season with salt and pepper, and continue to cook on a medium heat for a further 10 minutes.

Drain the cooked pasta, reserving some of the pasta water, and add to the sauce, mixing well. Allow it to infuse with the other ingredients for a couple of minutes. If it seems a little dry, add some pasta water to loosen the sauce.

Remove from the heat and serve with a drizzle of olive oil and the rest of the rosemary.

Insalata di pasta con pesto d'olive
Pasta salad with an olive pesto

350g/12oz fusilli

200g/7oz green beans, cooked until tender, drained and cooled

6 tomatoes, sliced

1 small yellow pepper, sliced

for the pesto

18 green olives, pitted

4 anchovy fillets, drained of their extra virgin olive oil

a little red chilli

handful of fresh parsley

180ml/12 tablespoons extra virgin olive oil, plus extra for drizzling (optional)

A simple pasta salad dressed with an olive pesto. Ideal for picnics, parties and lunch boxes, it can be made in advance and placed in the fridge until ready to serve. The olive pesto can also dress hot pasta.

Bring a large saucepan of slightly salted water to the boil, add the pasta and cook until *al dente*. Drain and leave to cool.

To make the pesto, place all the ingredients in a food processor and whiz slightly. Try not to let it become mushy – you want to maintain a little crunchiness. If you prefer, you can chop all the solid ingredients with a mezzaluna or sharp knife, then place in a bowl and stir in the olive oil.

Combine the cooled pasta with the green beans, tomatoes and yellow pepper in a large bowl. Add the pesto and mix well. Serve with a little drizzle of extra virgin olive oil, if desired.

Tip: When cooling the pasta, do not rinse under cold running water, just let it cool naturally. Rinsing it will remove all the salt that was added to the pasta water.

Pasta e fagioli
Pasta with beans

300g/10½oz tinned or dried cannellini or borlotti beans

1.5 litres/2¾ pints water

50g/1¾oz pancetta or bacon, finely chopped

1 garlic clove

4 cherry tomatoes, sliced in half or ½ tablespoon tomato purée

2 tablespoons parsley, roughly chopped

4 tablespoons extra virgin olive oil, plus extra for drizzling

300g/10½oz pasta shells, orecchiette or macaroni

salt and freshly ground black pepper

I have given you two versions of this very popular Italian dish, one using dried beans which you have to soak overnight and another for if you're in a hurry and want to use tinned. It's a really simple dish to prepare – it's all made in only one pot. It is a completely nutritious main course all on its own, without having to include any other dishes.

If you are using tinned beans, drain and place them in a saucepan with 1 litre/1¾ pints of the water.

Add the pancetta or bacon, garlic, tomatoes or purée, parsley, olive oil and season with salt. Bring to the boil, then leave to simmer gently for 5 minutes.

Add the pasta and continue to cook until *al dente*. Remove from the heat, stir in some freshly ground black pepper, then leave to rest for a couple of minutes. Serve with a drizzle of olive oil.

If you are making this with dried beans, soak them overnight, rinse and then cook according to the packet instructions. Fifteen minutes before the end of the suggested cooking time, add the pancetta, tomatoes or purée, parsley, garlic, olive oil and season with salt. Continue to simmer, partially covered, stirring from time to time. Finally, stir in the pasta and cook until *al dente*. Remove from the heat and serve as above.

Tip: For both methods, please ensure you have boiling water at the ready in case you need to add more during cooking, and please do add more at the end if you prefer a more soupy consistency.

Spaghetti alla carbonara
Spaghetti with egg and bacon sauce

350g/12oz long pasta, such as spaghetti, linguine or tagliatelle

4 eggs

100g/3½oz Parmesan cheese, freshly grated

100ml/3½fl oz milk

4 tbsp extra virgin olive oil

25g/1oz butter

120g/4¼oz pancetta or bacon

salt and pepper

Carbonara originated from the mountain region of Lazio where the carbonari *(charcoal burners) lived. This was a dish they would often eat. After World War II, Allied troops took this recipe back home since it used their favourite ingredients, eggs and bacon, and, of course, their new-found love, pasta! Over the years, different versions appeared, substituting milk for cream, adding herbs and garlic or onion. This is my version which resembles the original, except I now cook the eggs. Traditionally the cooked pasta was coated in raw beaten egg but I would recommend that everyone cooks them unless you are 100 per cent certain of where they come from.*

Place a large saucepan of slightly salted water on the heat to boil and cook the pasta until *al dente*.

Meanwhile, beat the eggs in a bowl with 50g/1¾oz of the Parmesan, the milk, some salt and pepper, and set aside.

In a large frying pan, heat the olive oil and butter, add the pancetta or bacon and stir-fry on a medium heat for about 4 minutes until golden and crispy.

Drain the pasta, reserving a little of the pasta water, and place it in the pan with the bacon and stir. Add the egg mixture and very quickly cook over the heat, coating the spaghetti with the egg and adding a little of the pasta water if it seems dry.

Remove from the heat and serve with the remaining Parmesan and freshly ground black pepper.

Farfalle con cipolla, pancetta e ricotta
Farfalle with onion, pancetta and ricotta

350g/12oz farfalle pasta

75ml/5 tablespoons extra virgin olive oil

4 sage leaves

3 medium onions, very finely chopped

3 slices pancetta or bacon, roughly chopped

300g/10½oz ricotta

50g/1¾oz pecorino cheese, freshly grated

salt and freshly ground black pepper

It is quite common to mix ricotta into a pasta sauce to make it a creamy dish. Here, I have added onions and pancetta but you could use peas or even a simple tomato sauce instead. Ricotta cheese is low-fat but nutritious and ideal for all the family to enjoy, from weaning babies to ladies on diets.

Bring a large saucepan of slightly salted water to the boil, add the pasta and cook until *al dente*.

Meanwhile, place the olive oil in a large frying pan over a high heat, and add the sage leaves, onion and pancetta or bacon. Reduce the heat to medium and sweat, stirring often to avoid sticking and burning.

Add about 4 tablespoons of the pasta water and the ricotta to the onion, mixing well to obtain a creamy consistency. Season with salt and pepper.

Drain the farfalle and add to the ricotta sauce. Stir in half of the grated pecorino and mix well.

Serve immediately with the rest of the pecorino cheese sprinkled on top and some freshly ground black pepper, if desired.

Pappardelle con porri, pancetta, arancia e noci
Pappardelle with leeks, pancetta, orange and walnuts

400g/14oz egg pappardelle

1½ oranges, zest of 1 removed and sliced into strips

100g/3½oz butter

180g/6¼oz pancetta or bacon, cubed

4 small leeks or 2 large leeks, cleaned and sliced into rounds

200ml/7fl oz white wine

100g/3½oz shelled walnuts, half finely chopped and half left whole

80g/3oz Parmesan cheese, freshly grated

salt and freshly ground black pepper

This is an up-to-date version of the traditional pasta with walnuts, in which I've added the delicate flavour of orange and the sweetness of leeks. An egg pasta such as pappardelle is ideal for this type of sauce. This is quick and simple to make, so why not treat the family to something different?

Place a large saucepan of slightly salted water on the heat to boil and cook the pasta until *al dente*.

While the pasta water is heating up, juice the oranges and pour this into a small pan. Bring to the boil and add the orange zest strips. Continue to cook until all the juice has evaporated, stirring to avoid sticking. This cooks the zest so it isn't bitter.

Meanwhile, melt the butter in a large frying pan on a medium heat. Add the pancetta or bacon and fry for a minute or two.

Add the leeks and stir-fry for a minute. Pour in the wine and partially cover with a lid. Cook for 5 minutes, stirring from time to time until most of the wine has evaporated.

Add the orange strips and the walnuts to the leeks, and mix well, adding some of the hot pasta water to make the sauce creamier. Continue to cook for a further minute so that all the flavours infuse. Add salt and lots of freshly ground black pepper to taste.

Drain the pappardelle and add to the sauce. Sprinkle with the Parmesan and mix well. Serve immediately.

Cavatelli con le cozze
Cavatelli with mussels

800g/1lb 12oz fresh mussels in their shells

90ml/6 tablespoons extra virgin olive oil

1 fillet of anchovy, finely chopped

1 tablespoon capers, finely chopped

3 garlic cloves, finely chopped

1 x 410g tin of plum tomatoes, chopped

½ teaspoon oregano

¼ red chilli, finely chopped

300g/10½oz cavatelli pasta

handful of fresh parsley, finely chopped

salt

When cooked, mussels exude a lot of liquid and, when combined with the tomatoes, this sauce becomes delicious and soupy. The mussels are cooked in the tomato sauce as well as their own juices, which adds to the taste. The pasta is finished in the same sauce so that it benefits from all flavours, too. Make sure you have some good bread to serve alongside so that when you have finished eating the pasta, you can dip some bread in the leftover sauce. If you can't find cavatelli, you can use orecchiette.

Clean the mussels under cold running water, removing the hairy 'beards' and discard any that have broken shells.

Heat the olive oil in a pan. Add the anchovy, capers and garlic, and sweat. Add the chopped tomatoes, oregano, chilli and mussels. Stir well, partially cover with a lid and cook on a medium heat for 20 minutes.

Meanwhile, cook the pasta in slightly salted boiling water until almost *al dente*.

Remove the opened mussels (keeping a few in their shells to garnish) and discard the shells. Discard any mussels that haven't opened. Return the shelled mussels to the sauce.

Drain the pasta, reserving a little of the pasta water, and place it in the tomato and mussel sauce. If the sauce is too thick, add some pasta water. Continue to cook the pasta in the sauce until it is *al dente*.

Serve immediately, sprinkled with the parsley and garnished with a few of the unshelled mussels.

Linguine con ragu bianco
Linguine with mince

360g/12½oz long pasta, such as tagliatelle, linguine or spaghetti

75ml/5 tablespoons extra virgin olive oil

1 large garlic clove, very finely chopped

1 bay leaf

350g/12oz steak mince

½ carrot, very finely chopped or grated

100ml/3½fl oz white wine

small handful of fresh parsley, finely chopped

40g/1½oz pecorino or Parmesan cheese, freshly grated

salt and pepper

Traditional Bolognese sauce is simple to make but takes about 2 hours to cook. Therefore here is the Italian housewife's quick alternative which does not include tomato and only takes about 5 minutes to make. For this recipe, it is best to get really good-quality, organic steak mince.

Bring a large saucepan of slightly salted water to the boil and cook the pasta until *al dente*.

Meanwhile, heat the olive oil, garlic and bay leaf in a frying pan and sweat the garlic. Reduce the heat to medium, add the mince and carrot, and cook for about 8 minutes, stirring all the time, until the meat is nearly cooked.

Pour in the wine, add the parsley, season with salt and pepper, and continue stirring until the wine has evaporated.

Drain the cooked pasta and add to the meat sauce with a couple of tablespoons of the pasta water. Mix well, sauté for a minute, remove from the heat and serve immediately with the grated cheese.

Tip: Ensure that the mince does not get too dry while cooking. If necessary, add more pasta water.

Tagliatelle con trota affumicata
Tagliatelle with smoked trout and wild fennel

350g/12oz egg tagliatelle

90ml/6 tablespoons extra virgin olive oil

1 small onion, finely chopped

1 garlic clove, finely chopped

½ tablespoon capers

½ glass white wine

200g/7oz tinned or fresh chopped plum tomatoes

handful of wild fennel, roughly chopped

200g/7oz smoked trout, roughly chopped

pinch of chilli powder (optional)

salt and pepper

This is a light, fresh-tasting pasta dish of smoked trout and wild fennel. Either pick your own fennel, or find it in the fresh herbs department of larger supermarkets. The trout can be replaced by smoked salmon, if you prefer.

Bring a large saucepan of slightly salted water to the boil, add the pasta and cook until *al dente*.

Meanwhile, place the olive oil in a large frying pan over a medium heat and sweat the onion, garlic and capers.

Turn up the heat, pour in the wine and allow to evaporate.

Reduce the heat to medium and stir in the tomatoes and half of the fennel. Season with salt and pepper and leave to simmer gently for 10 minutes.

Add the trout, stir through, and continue to simmer for another minute or so.

Drain the tagliatelle, reserving some of the pasta water, and stir into the sauce. Add a couple of tablespoons of the pasta water if it needs loosening. Mix well, remove from the heat, sprinkle with chilli powder, if using, and serve with the remaining fennel scattered on top.

Tip: If you can't find wild fennel, use the hairy fronds of a traditional fennel instead – or, for a slightly different flavour, you could also use dill.

Fusilli lunghi al tonno
Long fusilli with tuna

350g/12oz fusilli bucati

75ml/5 tablespoons extra virgin olive oil

1 medium red onion, finely chopped

2 small courgettes, finely cubed

1 carrot, finely cubed

½ red pepper, finely cubed

1 garlic clove, finely chopped

handful of fresh parsley, finely chopped

1 x 185g tin of tuna, drained and flaked

salt and pepper

A simple and nutritious pasta dish with vegetables and tuna – a perfect quick midweek meal for all the family. If you can't find fusilli bucati, go for another long pasta, such as spaghetti.

Place a large saucepan of slightly salted water on the heat to boil and cook the pasta until *al dente*.

Meanwhile, heat the olive oil in a pan, and add the onion, courgette, carrot and red pepper. Sweat on a medium heat for a couple of minutes, stirring all the time. Season with salt, add the garlic and parsley, and continue to cook for a further couple of minutes.

Drain the pasta and add to the vegetables, mixing well. Finally, stir in the tuna and serve immediately with some freshly ground black pepper, if desired.

Penne al cavalfiore e salsiccia
Penne with cauliflower and sausage

1 medium cauliflower, cleaned and cut into florets

350g/12oz short pasta, such as penne

75ml/5 tablespoons extra virgin olive oil

1 small onion, finely chopped

1 small carrot, finely chopped

½ celery stalk, finely chopped

1 bay leaf

200g/7oz pork sausages, roughly chopped

½ glass red wine

50g/1¾oz pecorino or Parmesan cheese, 20g/¾oz grated and the rest shavings

salt and pepper

This simple nutritious pasta dish is a meal in itself. The cauliflower combines really well with the sausage, but if you don't have any sausage, you can use bacon instead.

Place the cauliflower in a saucepan of slightly salted water and bring to the boil.

Add the pasta and cook until the cauliflower is tender and the pasta *al dente*. When they are ready, drain and set aside, reserving a little of the pasta water.

Meanwhile, heat the olive oil in a large frying pan, and add the onion, carrot, celery and bay leaf. Reduce the heat to medium and stir-fry for a few minutes until soft.

Stir in the sausage and cook for a couple of minutes to allow the flavours to infuse.

Pour in the wine and a couple of tablespoons of the pasta water, and season with salt and pepper. Allow to cook on a gentle heat for about 10 minutes.

Add the cauliflower and pasta to the sausage sauce, increase the heat and mix well, adding some more pasta water, if necessary. Mix in the grated cheese and then remove from the heat.

Serve immediately with shavings of cheese on top.

Tip: To avoid the odour of cauliflower when cooking, add a few bay leaves to the cooking water.

Main Courses

The main meal in Italy has always traditionally been at lunchtime and I remember that is how it was when I was a little boy. The typical midday meal consists of a primo (first course) of pasta, risotto or soup, followed by a secondo (main course) of meat or fish, and some vegetables or salad, followed by fruits of the season as a dessert. In the evening, the meal is a much lighter affair, usually a broth-type soup followed by some prosciutto or cheese and vegetables.

This tradition is gradually changing as more and more people live and work in the large cities and lunch breaks are just an hour long, as opposed to the three hours in the old days when everyone went home for a proper lunch and perhaps even a snooze! Nowadays, people tend to grab a sandwich and eat their main meal in the evening when everyone has returned home. In the evening Italians prefer to eat more lightly, so the trend is now for a one-course meal which includes all the necessary nutrients and vitamins. In smaller towns and villages, and among the older generation, the main meal is still three courses at lunchtime, though.

Whichever way you eat, whether you prefer a large lunch and lighter evening meal or vice versa, I hope you will find lots of quick and simple ideas among the following recipes. I have tried to include a variety of meat, fish and vegetarian options to satisfy all tastes. You will note I have included quite a few fish dishes – this is because fish is very quick to cook, as well as being healthy, so ideal to make after a day's work. I love cooking fish baked in a parcel (see page 94) – all the flavours infuse together nicely and the baking paper prevents the intense heat of the oven from overheating the fish and ruining its delicate flavour. Make sure you wrap up the fish and other ingredients gently, leaving space inside so that the steam which is formed can stay inside and not evaporate in the oven.

Risotto and gnocchi dishes are also quick, easy and nourishing, and it is always worth keeping a supply of risotto rice and a packet or two of fresh gnocchi in your larder. If you have your own ready-made tomato or pesto sauce, then adding some gnocchi really is an extremely quick meal which is nourishing and satisfying – fast food at its best!

Risotto
Basic risotto

1.5 litres/2¾ pints stock

3 tablespoons olive oil

1 medium onion, finely chopped

375g/13oz Arborio rice

50g/1¾oz butter

50g/1¾oz Parmesan cheese, grated

The first basic rule of making risotto is to use the correct Italian rice, such as Arborio, Carnaroli or Vialone Nano. Do not be tempted to use any other types as the risotto will not work. Next, use good stock – homemade is ideal but a good-quality cube or powder will suffice. The flavour of stock that you use will vary depending on the risotto you are making. For a basic risotto, I would use vegetable or chicken stock. Thirdly, keep the stock simmering gently on the heat while you are adding it to the rice, as it must be hot when it is added or the risotto will stop cooking and the dish will be ruined. And make sure all the liquid has been absorbed before adding more. The quantity of stock I have used for this recipe is correct but you may find you need more or less, so always have extra bubbling in your pan. Fourthly, you must keep stirring the risotto while it cooks or it may stick to the pan. And make sure it is on a low heat! Finally, once it is cooked, the risotto pan must be taken off the heat before you add the butter and Parmesan.

If you follow these few simple rules then there is no reason why you can't make your own tasty and filling risotto.

Make up the stock or place your own in a saucepan and leave it gently simmering on a low heat.

In a medium-sized, heavy-based saucepan, heat the olive oil and sweat the onion. Stir in the rice with a wooden spoon and coat each grain with the oil. Add a couple of ladles of the stock to the rice and, stirring all the time, cook until the stock is absorbed. Add more stock and stir. Continue to do this until the rice is cooked, which usually takes about 20 minutes. Taste the rice to check if it is ready – it should be soft on the outside but *al dente* inside.

Remove from the heat and, with a wooden spoon, beat in the butter and Parmesan so the risotto becomes well amalgamated and creamy. In Italy, this procedure is known as *mantecare*. Serve immediately.

Risotto al limone e ricotta
Lemon and ricotta risotto

2 tablespoons extra virgin olive oil

25g/1oz butter

1 small onion, very finely chopped

375g/13oz Arborio rice

1.5 litre/2¾ pints hot vegetable stock

zest of 1 lemon

juice of ½ lemon

150g/5½oz ricotta

a few marjoram or thyme leaves

salt and pepper

The secret of this recipe is a good lemon! Try to get one of the unwaxed, large varieties with a slightly thicker skin. If you can't, you may need the juice of another lemon to give the risotto a lemony taste. The addition of ricotta makes this risotto light and delicate and perfect for a quick meal.

Heat the olive oil and butter in a saucepan and sweat the onion. Reduce the heat to medium, add the rice and stir until each grain is coated with oil.

Add a couple of ladlefuls of stock and cook, stirring all the time, until it has been absorbed. Add about a quarter of the lemon zest and the lemon juice, season with salt and pepper, and stir.

Continue to add the stock a little at a time until the rice is *al dente*.

Remove from the heat, stir in the ricotta and about half of the marjoram or thyme leaves, and leave to rest for 1 minute.

Serve sprinkled with the remaining lemon zest and herbs.

Pane cotto con verdure
Stewed vegetables with poached egg and bread

4 tablespoons extra virgin olive oil, plus extra for drizzling

1 medium onion, finely chopped

200g/7oz fresh peas

100g/3½oz fresh broad beans

1 bunch of Swiss chard, roughly chopped

1 litre/1¾ pints hot vegetable stock

4 slices of stale country bread

4 eggs

50g/1¾oz pecorino, freshly grated

freshly ground black pepper

This is an old recipe which used to be made with broth and perhaps onion, tomato and stale bread. However, as with many recipes, this one has evolved to make it richer by adding a variety of vegetables and a poached egg. It is a nutritious meal in itself and perfect for vegetarians. If you wish, replace the vegetables suggested here with any that you prefer.

Heat the olive oil in a saucepan and sweat the onion. Stir in the peas, broad beans and Swiss chard and cook on a medium heat for a minute. Add the hot stock and some pepper, and simmer on a gentle heat for about 10–15 minutes until all the vegetables become tender.

Meanwhile, arrange the bread in 4 individual bowls. Poach the eggs one at a time in the pan with the stewed vegetables. The yolk should be set but still soft, so only leave them for a couple of minutes. Carefully remove with a slotted spoon and place one on each slice of bread.

Remove the vegetables from the heat and place around the eggs and bread. Drizzle with a little extra virgin olive oil and sprinkle with the grated pecorino cheese. Serve immediately.

Pollo cacciato
Chicken with tomato and mushrooms

100ml/8 tablespoons olive oil

1 onion, finely chopped

1 garlic clove, finely chopped

2 celery stalks, roughly chopped

1 carrot, roughly chopped

2 bay leaves

4 sage leaves

1kg/2lb 4oz chicken, cut into bite-sized chunks

1 glass white wine

100g/3½oz button mushrooms

1 x 410g tin of plum tomatoes, chopped

some hot vegetable or chicken stock, if needed

salt and pepper

This classic Italian dish was one of my mother's favourites and we would often eat this as a weekday meal. It used to feature on a lot of Italian restaurant menus abroad, but it was so badly made that I don't blame people for complaining and gradually it fell out of fashion. It's a shame because when made properly, it is a really delicious dish and is so easy to prepare.

Heat the olive oil in a saucepan and sweat the onion, garlic, celery, carrot, bay leaves and sage.

Add the chicken pieces and seal well on all sides. Season with salt and pepper, add the wine and allow to evaporate.

Stir in the mushrooms and tomatoes, and bring to the boil. Turn down the heat, partially cover with a lid and simmer on a medium heat for 30 minutes until the chicken has cooked. Check from time to time and if it is looking a little bit dry, add some hot stock.

Serve with rice, polenta or simply some good bread.

Frittata di verdure al forno
Baked vegetable omelette

50g/1¾oz butter, plus extra for greasing

2 tablespoons extra virgin olive oil

300g/10½oz spinach, roughly chopped

150g/5½oz fresh or frozen peas

6 eggs

100g/3½oz hard mozzarella, finely chopped

50g/1¾oz mortadella, cubed

salt and pepper

A healthier way of cooking an omelette and it avoids the problem of flipping it over! Usually I make this dish with one of my favourite vegetables, escarole, but I have put spinach in this recipe because it's easier to find. You can, of course, include other vegetables if you prefer, and use different cheese and ham if you don't like mortadella. It is an easy and quick complete meal for all the family.

Pre-heat the oven to 180°C/350°F/Gas 4.

Heat the butter and olive oil in a frying pan and add the spinach. Cook on a medium heat for about 2–3 minutes until it has softened.

Add the peas and a couple of tablespoons of water, cover with a lid and continue to cook on a low heat for a further 5 minutes until the peas have softened, too.

Remove from the heat and leave to cool slightly.

In a bowl, beat the eggs with some salt and pepper, stir in the mozzarella, mortadella and the cooled vegetables.

Lightly grease an ovenproof dish (approx. 22cm/8½in diameter) with some butter, pour in the mixture and bake in the pre-heated oven for about 20–25 minutes until the omelette has set and is golden.

Remove from the oven, leave to rest for a minute, then serve hot or cold.

Lasagna vegetariana
Vegetable lasagne

90ml/6 tablespoons oil for frying and greasing

1 red pepper, sliced in strips

1 courgette, cut into rounds

1 small aubergine, cubed

1 quantity of Basic White Sauce (see page 168)

1 tablespoon onion, very finely chopped

500ml/18fl oz tomato passata

handful of fresh basil

approx. 8 dried lasagne sheets – the quantity depends upon the size of your dish and how many layers you make

180g/6¼oz hard mozzarella, roughly chopped

20g/¾oz Parmesan cheese, freshly grated

salt and pepper

A lasagne always seems such a time-consuming recipe, but this one really is not. If you are organized and make the white sauce while the vegetables are cooking, then you are halfway there. This type of vegetarian lasagne is very simple to prepare and is made in the same way as the classic Emilian lasagne, replacing the meat with vegetables. I like to make a tomato sauce and mix it with the vegetables to make the dish more gooey. However, you could omit the tomato and just use vegetables and white sauce.

Pre-heat the oven to 200°C/400°F/Gas 6.

Heat the oil in a pan and sauté the vegetables over a medium heat until soft. Meanwhile, make the white sauce (seen page 172).

Take the vegetables out of the pan and place on kitchen paper to remove excess oil and set aside.

Pour most of the oil out of the pan and put back on a medium heat. Sweat the onion and then add the tomato passata and cook for 5 minutes.

Remove from the heat, add the cooked vegetables, basil, season with salt and pepper, and set aside.

Lightly grease an ovenproof dish with some oil. Line the dish with a little of the tomato sauce (not including any vegetables). Arrange a layer of lasagne sheets over the top, then a layer of white sauce. Next, put a layer of tomato and vegetable sauce, including the vegetables this time, and sprinkle with some mozzarella, Parmesan and some freshly ground black pepper. Continue with another layer of lasagne sheets and then all the following layers until all the ingredients have been used. Make sure to end with a topping of cheese.

Cover with aluminium foil and bake in the oven for 15 minutes. Remove the aluminium foil and continue to bake for a further 15 minutes until golden and cooked through.

Remove from the oven, leave to rest for a minute or so and serve.

Gnocchi con verdure
Gnocchi with peas, asparagus and leek

2 tablespoons extra virgin olive oil

1 leek, finely chopped

100g/3½oz fresh or frozen peas

100g/3½oz asparagus tips

80g/3oz butter

a few sage leaves

needles of 1 rosemary branch

a few basil leaves

800g/1lb 12oz ready-made potato gnocchi

30g/1oz Parmesan cheese, freshly grated

salt

Although I love to make my own potato gnocchi, time does not always allow it. The ready-made varieties are getting better all the time and, combined with a good sauce, make for a quick and nourishing meal. The gnocchi is cooked in the vegetable water to give the dish extra flavour and the addition of herbs to the melted butter provides a wonderful aroma and taste.

Heat the olive oil in a pan, add the leek and sauté until soft. Set aside.

Place a saucepan of slightly salted water on the heat and bring to the boil. Add the peas and asparagus tips, and cook for 3 minutes until the vegetables are tender. Remove with a slotted spoon and set aside.

Bring the vegetable water back to the boil.

Meanwhile, melt the butter in a frying pan, add the herbs and allow to infuse for a couple of minutes.

As the water boils, drop in the gnocchi and cook until they float to the surface.

Remove the gnocchi with a slotted spoon and place in a serving dish. Top with the leeks, peas and asparagus, and then pour over the hot herby butter. Carefully mix together, taking care not the break the asparagus tips, sprinkle with the Parmesan and serve immediately.

Crespelle con ricotta e rucola
Baked filled savoury pancakes

250g/9oz plain flour
4 eggs
500ml/18fl oz milk
40g/1½oz butter, melted, plus extra for greasing and dotting
20g/¾oz Parmesan cheese, freshly grated
½ quantity of Tomato Sauce, using onion (see page 165)
salt

for the filling

300g/10½oz ricotta
100g/3½oz rocket, finely chopped, plus some unchopped for garnishing
50g/1¾oz Parmesan cheese, freshly grated
salt and pepper

1 × 16cm/6¼in non-stick frying pan

Crespelle *are the Italian equivalent of pancakes. The pancake itself is made in the same way as an English one, but they are then filled with a savoury mixture and baked and served with tomato sauce. Simple to prepare, they make a different and nutritious meal. I have opted for a ricotta and rocket filling, but you can make any filling you like – try spinach, mixed vegetables, mushrooms or even make them sweet for dessert.*

Sift the flour and a pinch of salt into a bowl, add the eggs and stir. Gradually whisk in the milk, ensuring no lumps are formed, until you obtain a smooth runny batter, then stir in the melted butter.

Place the frying pan on the heat, grease with a little butter, then add a ladleful of the mixture in the centre of the pan. Swirl the pan around so that the mixture runs to all sides. Fry until the bottom is golden, then flip over to cook on the other side. Remove and set aside. Continue to do this until your mixture has finished – you should be able to make 8 pancakes.

Pre-heat the oven to 190°C/375°F/Gas 5.

To make the filling, combine all the ingredients, mixing well.

Spread some of the filling on to each pancake, then fold each one in half and half again, ending up with a triangle. Place on a greased ovenproof dish so that they slightly overlap each other, dot with knobs of butter and sprinkle with the Parmesan. Bake in the oven for 10 minutes.

Remove and top with a spoonful of tomato sauce on each pancake. Garnish with some rocket and serve.

Sogliole dorate alle erbe
Sole fillets with a herb crust

80g/3oz breadcrumbs

needles of 1 rosemary branch, finely chopped

20 sage leaves, finely chopped

1 teaspoon fennel seeds

freshly ground black pepper

1kg/2lb 4oz sole fillets

abundant oil for frying

Really quick and simple to prepare, the breadcrumb mixture includes herbs and fennel that give a wonderful aroma to the fish. This dish is ideally served with a cherry tomato salad. You can use other fillets of fish such as cod or halibut if sole is unavailable.

Combine the breadcrumbs, herbs, fennel seeds and black pepper, and coat the sole fillets with this mixture, pressing well so it sticks to the fish.

Heat about 6 tablespoons of oil in a large frying pan, add the sole fillets and fry on both sides until golden. (Depending on how absorbent the breadcrumbs are, you may need to add some more oil before you turn the fillets over.)

Trota alle erbe aromatiche miste
Trout fillets baked with mixed herbs

3 dessertspoonfuls mixed fresh herbs – e.g. parsley, tarragon and chives, roughly chopped

2 garlic cloves, finely chopped

4 trout fillets, weighing approx. 200g/7oz each

4 tablespoons extra virgin olive oil

4 lemon wedges

salt and pepper

4 sheets of baking/parchment paper, big enough to wrap around a fish

Very simple and quick to make, with an amazing aroma of delicately cooked trout and herbs once you unwrap the parcel.

Pre-heat the oven to 180°C/350°F/Gas 4.

Combine the herbs and garlic. Place each fish fillet in the centre of a sheet of baking paper, sprinkle with the herbs and garlic, season with salt and pepper, and drizzle with the olive oil.

Wrap the baking paper around the fish, sealing well. Place in the pre-heated oven for 15 minutes.

Remove from the oven. Leave to rest for a few minutes, then carefully open each parcel and serve immediately with some lemon wedges.

Merluzzo con pomodoro e fagioli bianchi
Cod with tomato and butter beans

180ml/12 tablespoons extra virgin olive oil

1 leek, finely chopped

250g/9oz tinned butter beans, well drained

1 x 410g tin of chopped plum tomatoes,

400ml/16fl oz hot vegetable stock

4 slices of cod, weighing approx. 250g/9oz each

plain flour for coating

handful of fresh parsley, finely chopped

salt and pepper

A quick and simple way to cook cod, making this an ideal midweek dinner for all the family. Just serve with bread for a complete meal.

Heat 4 tablespoons of the olive oil in a pan and sweat the leeks. Stir in the beans and chopped tomatoes. Add the hot vegetable stock and salt to taste. Gently simmer for 10 minutes.

Coat the cod slices in the flour. In another pan, heat the remaining olive oil and add the fish. Fry on both sides until cooked and golden.

With a fish slice, carefully remove the cod and add to the beans and tomato sauce. Grind over some black pepper and continue to cook on a medium heat covered with a lid for a further 4 minutes.

Remove from the heat, add some chopped parsley and serve.

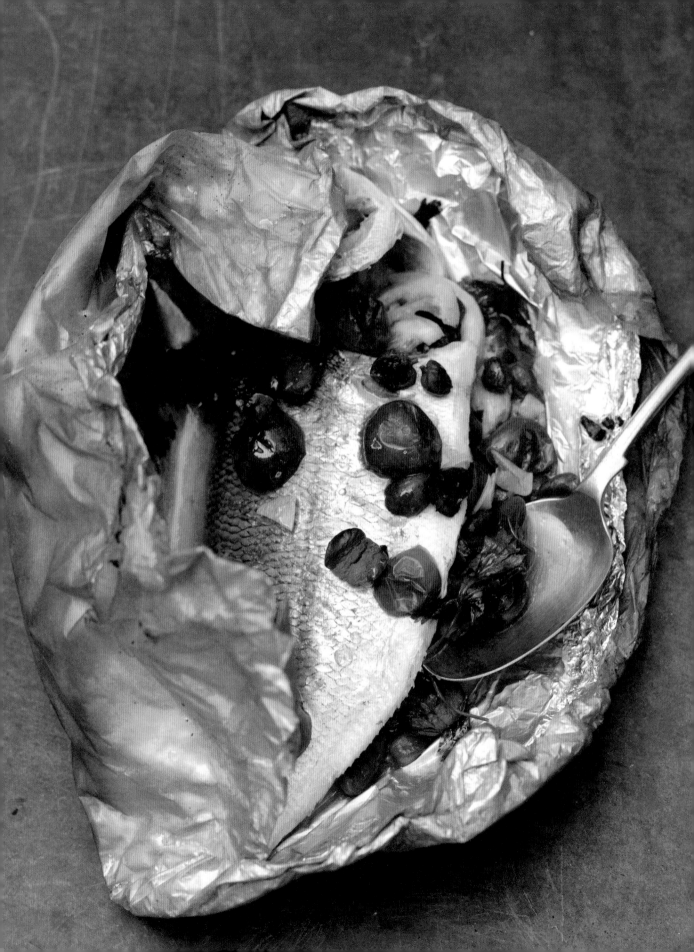

Orate al cartoccio
Steamed baked seabream

4 seabream, weighing approx. 250g/9oz each, descaled and slit along the belly

20 black olives, pitted

2 garlic cloves, sliced

1 bunch of fresh parsley, roughly chopped

16 cherry tomatoes, halved or quartered

90ml/6 tablespoons extra virgin olive oil

salt and pepper

4 sheets of baking/parchment paper, big enough to wrap around a fish

This is the very taste of the Mediterranean and is based upon Orata all'acqua pazza, although the original recipe is cooked in a pan. I love seabream cooked with these few simple ingredients, which are so reminiscent of childhood days in Italy by the coast. In this recipe, all the flavours are trapped in the baking paper and when you unwrap the parcel the aroma is amazing! Be careful of the steam, though. Open a little gap in the paper at first and then, as the steam comes out, gradually open it fully. This is great served with boiled new potatoes and some fresh green vegetables.

Pre-heat the oven to 180°C/350°F/Gas 4.

Rinse the fish under cold running water and pat dry. Place each fish in the centre of a sheet of baking paper. In each belly, place a few olives, some slices of garlic, some parsley, and season with salt and pepper. Scatter the tomatoes over the fish and drizzle with the olive oil.

Close the baking paper around each fish, ensuring that you seal it well. Place in the pre-heated oven for about 25 minutes until the fish has cooked through.

Remove from the oven, leave to rest for a couple of minutes, unwrap and serve – either place the parcels on individual serving plates and let everyone help themselves or remove the fish very carefully with a fish slice and place on to plates, pouring over the juices.

Galletti ripieni con patate novelle
Roast baby chickens with new potatoes

2 whole baby chickens

4 slices streaky bacon

olive oil for greasing

1kg/2lb 4oz baby new potatoes, unpeeled, left whole and par-boiled for 5 minutes

a few rosemary needles

½ glass white wine

salt and pepper

for the filling

200g/7oz tinned sweetcorn, drained

200g/7oz stale bread, softened in milk and strained

80g/3oz Parma ham, finely chopped

40g/1½oz Parmesan cheese, freshly grated

2 sage leaves, finely chopped

salt and pepper

kitchen string

Baby chickens are so much nicer to look at and easier to carve than normal-sized chickens. One baby chicken feeds 2 people. As a young boy, I remember our chickens were fed on corn and when I first came to England, it surprised me to see people eating corn. After trying it myself, though, I realized how delicious it was. This is what gave me the idea to use sweetcorn in the filling.

Pre-heat the oven to 220°C/425°F/Gas 7.

Make the filling by combining all the ingredients together well. Stuff the baby chickens with this filling. Top the chickens with the bacon and tie well with string so the filling does not escape.

Place in a well-oiled roasting tin together with the parboiled potatoes. Sprinkle with the rosemary needles, season with salt and pepper, and drizzle with some olive oil.

Add the wine, cover with foil and roast in the oven for approximately 15 minutes. Remove the foil and continue to roast for 25 minutes until the chickens are cooked through.

Remove from the oven, leave to rest for a minute, then serve.

Pollo e patate al forno
Italian chicken hotpot

4 chicken quarters

1kg/2lb 4oz potatoes, peeled and cut into ½ cm/¼in slices

60g/2¼oz pitted black olives

1 tablespoon capers

½ teaspoon oregano

needles of 1 rosemary branch

50g/1¾oz pancetta or bacon, roughly chopped

½ glass white wine

½ glass water

90ml/6 tablespoons extra virgin olive oil

salt and pepper

Pollo e patate *(chicken and potatoes) is a much-cooked and much-loved dish in Italy. I suppose it is like having roast chicken with roast potatoes for Sunday lunch in England! That is what I have based this recipe on, but here I have used chicken quarters and the aroma of the Mediterranean.*

Pre-heat the oven to 200°C/400°F/Gas 6.

In a large bowl place all the ingredients and mix well together. Remove the chicken quarters and set aside.

Line an ovenproof dish with a layer of potatoes and other ingredients. Place the chicken quarters on top. Then cover with the remaining potatoes and other ingredients.

Cover with foil and place in the oven for about 20 minutes. Remove the foil and continue to cook for a further 20 minutes until the the top layer of potatoes are golden and the chicken is cooked through.

Involtini di tacchino
Filled turkey rolls

4 slices of turkey breast, weighing approx. 200g/7oz each

plain flour, for dusting

4 tablespoons extra virgin olive oil

1 garlic clove

needles of 2 rosemary branches

120ml/4fl oz white wine

salt and pepper

for the filling

4 plum tomatoes, deseeded, drained of liquid and roughly chopped

100g/3½oz hard mozzarella, roughly chopped

6 black pitted olives, finely chopped

handful of basil leaves, torn into strips

kitchen string and/or cocktail sticks for securing

Involtini di carne (meat rolls) were nearly always served for Sunday lunch at home in Italy, usually filled with bits of leftover sausages, cheese and herbs. I like to experiment and these are a more up-to-date version – lighter and more delicate but just as tasty. They are delicious served with Green Bean Salad (see page 125).

Flatten the turkey slices to about ½cm/¼in thick and sprinkle a little salt and pepper all over.

Combine all the filling ingredients. Divide into 4 portions and place one portion on each turkey slice. Carefully roll and tie with string or secure with cocktail sticks. Ensure that the filling does not escape. Lightly dust each roll with some flour.

Heat the olive oil in a pan over a high heat. Add the garlic, rosemary and the filled turkey rolls and seal the meat well on all sides. Add the wine, reduce the heat to medium, cover with a lid and cook for about 10–15 minutes until the turkey is cooked through.

Remove from the heat and serve immediately.

Spezzatino di maiale al pomodoro
Pork stew with tomatoes

90ml/6 tablespoons extra virgin olive oil

3 shallots, finely chopped

1 carrot, finely chopped

2 celery stalks, finely chopped

50g/1¾oz pancetta or bacon, finely chopped

800g/1lb 12oz stewing pork, cut into small cubes

plain flour for dusting

80ml/2½fl oz white wine

300g/10½oz tinned tomatoes, chopped

80ml/2½fl oz hot vegetable stock

4 medium potatoes, peeled and cut into small chunks

100g/3½oz fresh or frozen peas

a little parsley, finely chopped

salt and pepper

A quick, simple and nutritious stew, which is a meal in itself. Make sure the pork is cooked through. The smaller the chunks, the quicker the meat will cook.

Heat the olive oil in a large saucepan. Add the shallots, carrot, celery and pancetta or bacon and sweat on a medium heat.

Dust the pieces of pork in flour, shaking off the excess. Add the meat to the vegetables and seal on all sides.

Add the white wine and allow to evaporate.

Stir in the tomatoes and season with salt and pepper. Lower the heat and cover with a lid. Cook for 25 minutes, gradually adding the stock a little at a time, until the meat is cooked through. If you find the stew dries up, add a little more hot stock.

Add the potato chunks and peas and cook for a further 15 minutes, still on a low heat, stirring from time to time.

Remove from the heat, leave to rest for a minute, then stir in the parsley and serve.

Gnocchi al forno
Baked gnocchi with a cheese, ham and sage sauce

1 quantity of Basic White Sauce (see page 168)

150g/5½oz fontina cheese, roughly chopped

200g/7oz cooked ham, roughly chopped

30g/1oz butter, plus extra for greasing

6 sage leaves

600g/1lb 5oz ready-made potato gnocchi

100g/3½oz Parmesan cheese, freshly grated

salt and pepper

A simple meal that is both nutritious and satisfying. It can be made in advance and baked when required, which makes it even more appealing!

Pre-heat the oven to 200°C/400°F/Gas 6.

First prepare the white sauce. When it is ready, remove from the heat and stir in the fontina and ham. Set aside.

Bring a large saucepan of slightly salted water to the boil.

Meanwhile, heat the butter in a small pan, add the sage leaves and sauté for a minute.

Drop the gnocchi into the boiling water and when they float to the surface, take them out with a slotted spoon and add them to the pan of butter and sage, stirring well.

Lightly grease an ovenproof dish with some butter. Spread a little of the cheese and ham sauce on the base of the dish and add the rest to the cooked gnocchi, mixing well. Pour half of the gnocchi into the dish, sprinkle with some Parmesan, then pour in the remaining gnocchi and top with the remaining Parmesan.

Cover with a sheet of foil and bake in the pre-heated oven for 10 minutes. Remove the foil and continue to bake for a further 15 minutes until golden.

Take out of the oven, leave to rest for a couple of minutes and then serve.

Scaloppine di maiale al mandarino con porri
Pork with mandarin oranges, herbs and leeks

150g/5½oz plain flour

zest of ½ mandarin orange

6 sage leaves

1 bay leaf

1 small thyme branch

4 slices of thin pork escalope, weighing approx. 200g/7oz each

100g/3½oz butter

1 leek, sliced into rounds

1 mandarin orange, peeled and separated into segments

2 tablespoons white wine

juice of 4 mandarin oranges

salt and pepper

I would normally make this with veal, but since it isn't so widely available in England, I have opted for pork, which works just as well. I have based this dish on the classic Scaloppine al limone *(escalopes with lemon), using mandarins instead to give a sweet tang to the meat. Served with the leeks and some boiled potatoes, this makes a quick and delicious meal.*

Put the flour and mandarin zest into a food processor and whiz until you obtain a very fine consistency. Coat the pork with this mixture, pressing it well with your hands so that it sticks to the meat. Set aside.

Heat 30g/1oz of the butter in a frying pan over a medium heat. Add the leeks and mandarin segments and sauté for 4 minutes.

Remove the leeks and mandarin segments and set aside.

Heat the remaining butter in the pan, add the herbs and pork slices and fry on each side until golden. Return the leeks and mandarin segments to the pan, add the wine and allow to evaporate gently until the sauce has reduced by half.

Add the mandarin juice and continue to cook for 3 minutes. Season with salt and pepper, remove from the heat and serve.

Coniglio spezziato
Spicy roast chicken

6 chicken thighs

3 celery stalks, finely chopped

1 medium onion, finely chopped

3 garlic cloves

6 sage leaves

needles of 1 rosemary branch

2 red chillies, finely chopped

4 tablespoons extra virgin olive oil

2 teaspoons salt

1 glass white wine

juice of ½ lemon

handful of fresh parsley, finely chopped

Originally this recipe was a rabbit dish, but because of its lack of availability in UK shops I have substituted chicken for rabbit, which works just as well. Of course, if you fancy having rabbit, excellent fat-free white meat, then a good butcher will stock it. Ask for a whole rabbit cut into chunks.

In a bowl, place the chicken and all the other ingredients except for the lemon juice and parsley. Mix well, cover and leave to marinate for 10 minutes.

Place the chicken and marinade ingredients in a large pan and cook on a medium heat for about 10 minutes. Cover with a lid and continue to cook for a further 15–20 minutes, stirring and turning the meat over from time to time. If it is looking dry, add a little hot water. Five minutes before the end of the cooking time, drizzle with the lemon juice.

Remove from the heat, sprinkle with parsley and serve.

Arrosto di manzo con le erbe
Quick roast beef with herbs

100ml/8 tablespoons extra virgin olive oil

800g/1lb 12oz piece of boneless fore rib beef – ask your butcher to roll it flat

200ml/7fl oz red wine

150ml/5fl oz hot beef stock

needles of 1 rosemary branch

leaves of 2 thyme branches

3 bay leaves

coarse sea salt and freshly ground black pepper

The secret to this quick 'roast' beef is the quality of the meat, and I suggest you get this from a good butcher. This is a quick and delicious alternative to your usual Sunday roast beef and, in fact, because of the short cooking time, the meat is even more succulent. This would go nicely with the Roast Potatoes with Bay Leaves (see page 131).

In a large, non-stick pan with tall sides, heat the olive oil on a medium heat. Add the meat and seal well on all sides for about 5 minutes.

Add the red wine, followed by the hot stock. Stir in the herbs and continue to cook with a lid on for a further 20 minutes, turning the meat several times.

Season with salt and pepper, remove from the heat, slice the beef and serve immediately.

Costolette di agenello con susine speziate
Lamb cutlets with spicy plums

8 lamb cutlets

90ml/6 tablespoons extra virgin olive oil

2 medium onions, finely sliced

1 garlic clove, finely sliced

2cm/¾in piece of ginger, peeled and finely chopped

400g/14oz plums, pitted and cut in half

needles of 2 rosemary branches, roughly chopped

2 tablespoons runny honey

½ teaspoon ground cinnamon

½ teaspoon powdered cardamom

salt and pepper

Even though I don't really like including exotic spices in my recipes, I know I need to change with the times. Italians have finally discovered these spices and it's great – in fact, my sister, Adriana, has started selling exotic spices in her shop and business is booming!

Rub salt and pepper all over the lamb cutlets.

Heat the olive oil in a large frying pan, add the lamb cutlets and cook on both sides for 3 or 4 minutes. Remove and set aside.

In the same pan, stir-fry the onion, garlic and ginger for a minute. Add the plums, rosemary, honey, cinnamon and cardamom and cook on a medium heat covered with a lid for 8–10 minutes.

Stir in some salt and pepper, move the plums to one side of the pan and return the lamb cutlets to heat through for a minute or so, turning them over to flavour both sides.

Remove from the heat and serve with some steamed rice if desired.

Polpettine di carne
Meatballs

250g/9oz minced beef

250g/9oz minced pork

100g/3½oz stale bread, crusts removed and softened in a couple of tablespoons of milk, then drained

½ garlic clove, finely chopped

1 tablespoon parsley, finely chopped

1 egg

40g/1½oz Parmesan cheese, freshly grated

plain flour for dusting

oil (if you are frying)

salt and pepper

Meatballs are comfort food to me whether they are plain or served in a tomato sauce with pasta. I remember as a child, the meatballs never made it into the sauce because we children would steal them as they came out of the frying pan. Once you had eaten one, you just had to carry on, they were so tasty! But, if you do want to serve them with tomato sauce, use the recipe on page 165 and at the end of the cooking time add the meatballs and heat through gently for 10 minutes.

Combine the minced meats, softened bread, garlic and parsley. Stir in the egg, Parmesan, some salt and pepper and mix well together.

Shape the meat into small balls, approximately the size of walnuts. Dust them in flour and set aside.

You can now either fry them or bake them. To fry, heat the oil in a pan and fry the meatballs until golden. Drain on kitchen paper before serving. To bake, pre-heat the oven to 200°C/400°F/Gas 6 and cook the meatballs for about 20 minutes until golden.

Tip: You can also serve them on skewers. Alternate the meatballs with pieces of aubergine, courgette and peppers or simply with halved cherry tomatoes and basil leaves and bake them in the oven at 200°C/400°F/ Gas 6 for about 20 minutes. Serve with steamed rice and tomato sauce.

vegetables & Salads

I consider Italians very lucky to have such a vast selection of wonderful vegetables and salads. Each region has its own locally grown varieties which, in season, are excellent for the traditional dishes of that particular area. Italy is blessed with its Mediterranean climate and the difference between the cooler north and the warmer south makes it ideal for growing all sorts of different produce – the north with its root vegetables and the south with its tomatoes, peppers and aubergines.

Italians really look forward to the different seasons and the food they bring. The fresh asparagus, peas and broad beans in spring are a wonderful treat and it is a good time to cook as many dishes as possible with these vegetables. The same happens at the end of summer when tomatoes are plentiful and often they'll be preserved so that wonderful tomato sauces can be enjoyed later on in the year. It is a shame that nowadays more and more produce can be bought all year round. The joy of waiting for a certain vegetable to come into season is no longer there. But I take solace from all the people I know who grow their own vegetables and from those like my friend, Mike, who, despite working long hours, still finds time to go out and collect wild produce of the season. When I have time, I like to do the same with my family and, when I return to Minori, it pleases me to see that people are still buying seasonally and still enjoying preserving.

Italians don't just eat vegetables and salads as a side dish, but we make wonderful main course dishes out of them, too. We even use certain salad leaves in main courses; for example, the much-loved southern Italian escarole can be filled with leftover bits of bread, salami, herbs and cheese to make a most nutritious meal. Vegetables are so quick and easy to cook, they are full of goodness and there is always such a variety on offer at the market, that it is really tempting to buy lots. I would be perfectly happy to eat a plateful of delicious green vegetables, lightly cooked in extra virgin olive oil, chilli and garlic, and nothing else. Or perhaps a bowl of mixed pulses, a crunchy salad, or some sliced good tomatoes with extra virgin olive oil, salt and basil leaves, accompanied with some good bread. I often hear people complaining when they have vegetarians over for dinner, but it is never a problem for an Italian – the famous melanzana di parmigiana (a baked aubergine dish), for a start, is simple to make and very nutritious. There are delicious pasta and rice dishes you can make with lots of lovely seasonal vegetables, as well.

Most of the recipes I have included in this chapter can be eaten as a main course or as an accompaniment to other dishes. I hope you will enjoy making them and that you will share in my love of vegetables.

Insalata di mele
Apple salad

1 medium beetroot, precooked and sliced into thin strips

1 small carrot, sliced into shavings – best way to do this is with a peeler

1 small fennel, thinly sliced

1 small apple, peeled, cored, thinly sliced and drizzled with a little lemon juice to avoid discoloration

100g/3½oz baby salad leaves

50g/1¾oz flaked almonds, lightly toasted

for the dressing

20g/¾oz capers, plus extra for garnishing (optional)

2 fillets of anchovies

1 garlic clove, finely chopped

½ teaspoon horseradish sauce

2 cloves

pinch of chilli powder

80ml/2½fl oz extra virgin olive oil

1 tablespoon red wine vinegar

2 tablespoons lemon juice

salt and pepper

Please don't be put off by the long list of ingredients for the dressing: they are all things you can find in your store cupboard and, when combined, make a truly delicious dressing. The salad ingredients go very well together with their contrasting textures and tastes, and when served with the toasted almonds and dressing make for a lovely dish indeed.

Arrange the vegetables, apple and salad leaves on a large serving dish or in a salad bowl, sprinkling the toasted almonds over the top.

Make the salad dressing by placing all the ingredients and seasoning into a blender and whiz until you obtain a smooth consistency.

Drizzle the dressing over the salad and garnish with capers, if using. Leave to rest for a couple of minutes and then serve.

Cuscus di verdure
Couscous salad

300g/10½oz couscous

300ml/10fl oz hot vegetable stock

300g/10½oz mixture of red pepper, yellow pepper, spring onions, tomatoes, cucumber, courgette, all finely sliced

a few mint leaves, finely chopped

for the dressing

juice of ½ lemon

100ml/3½fl oz extra virgin olive oil

pinch of chilli powder

salt

Couscous was introduced to Italy by the North African countries via Sicily and Sardinia. It is made from semolina and is traditionally cooked for a long time. However, these days we are able to purchase the precooked variety, which only takes a few minutes to revive in hot liquid. Couscous is extremely easy to prepare, delicious with some vegetables added to it and dressed with extra virgin olive oil and lemon juice. I love to add a little chilli, too, for that extra kick! It is great served warm or cold as a side dish – perfect for parties or even as a quick lunch.

Put the couscous in a bowl, pour over the hot vegetable stock, cover and leave to absorb for a few minutes. (Check the instructions on the couscous packet as they do tend to differ slightly.)

Meanwhile, whisk all the dressing ingredients together.

Add the vegetables to the couscous, pour over the dressing, sprinkle with mint and mix well. Serve immediately or when required.

Insalata di legumi misti al pomodoro
Salad of mixed pulses with tomato and rocket

40g/1½oz fresh or frozen broad beans

40g/1½oz fresh or frozen peas

250g/9oz soaked and precooked or tinned mixed pulses, such as chickpeas, lentils, borlotti beans and black-eyed beans, well drained

4 salad tomatoes, deseeded and cut into small cubes

a bunch of rocket or mixed green leaves

4 spring onions, finely chopped

2 marjoram branches, leaves removed and stalks discarded

a few sage leaves

90ml/6 tablespoons extra virgin olive oil

3 tablespoons balsamic vinegar

salt and pepper

If you have time, do use dried pulses, which have been soaked overnight, then cooked. But, if you don't, then use tinned pulses, of which there are a huge variety in shops and supermarkets. In season, it is best to have fresh broad beans and peas, but the frozen varieties are an excellent substitute. This is a quick and simple salad, which is most nutritious.

Cook the broad beans and peas until tender. Drain and leave to cool.

Place the well-drained pulses, broad beans and peas in a large bowl or serving dish and add the tomatoes, spring onions, rocket and herbs.

Pour over the olive oil and vinegar, season with salt and pepper and mix everything together.

Leave to rest for 10 minutes, then serve.

Insalata di fagiolini
Green bean salad

300g/10½oz green beans, cooked until tender

4 salad tomatoes, sliced

600g/1lb 5oz baby new potatoes, unpeeled and cooked until tender

200g/7oz hard mozzarella, cubed

handful of green pitted olives

pinch of dried oregano

a few basil leaves

for the dressing

1 garlic clove, finely chopped

80ml/2½fl oz extra virgin olive oil

2 tablespoons white wine vinegar

salt and pepper

Green beans and potatoes go really well together. Here I have added a few more ingredients to make it a more complete meal. It makes an ideal side dish, main dish for a light supper, and is great for parties or barbeques.

Place the green beans, tomatoes, potatoes, mozzarella, olives and oregano in a large bowl.

Make the dressing by whisking all the ingredients together until you obtain a smooth creamy consistency. Pour over the vegetables and top with a few basil leaves.

Toss well, leave to rest for a few minutes and serve.

Ciambotta di verdure
Italian mixed vegetables

abundant oil for frying

3 medium potatoes, peeled and cut into bite-sized chunks

1 courgette, sliced into rounds

½ red pepper, roughly sliced into strips

½ yellow pepper, roughly sliced into strips

1 small aubergine, cut into small cubes

2 tablespoons extra virgin olive oil

½ onion, finely chopped

200g/7oz tinned plum tomatoes, chopped

handful of basil leaves

30g/1oz Parmesan cheese, freshly grated

salt and pepper

You may be put off this recipe because of the frying, but please don't be! The vegetables are only lightly fried in good oil then drained well – I assure you they will not taste fatty. Try this as something different to accompany meat or even as a main dish, served with steamed rice. You could also follow this recipe, excluding the potato, to make the vegetables for the Vegetable Lasagne (see page 84).

Heat 6 tablespoons of oil in a pan. When hot, add the potatoes and cook until golden. Remove, drain on kitchen paper and set aside. Heat more oil in the pan, if necessary, then fry the courgette, drain and set aside. Do the same with the peppers and finally the aubergines. Season all the vegetables with salt and pepper.

Heat the olive oil in another pan, add the onion and sweat over a medium heat. Stir in the tomatoes and season with some salt and pepper, cover with a lid and cook for 10 minutes.

Combine the fried vegetables with the tomato sauce, stir in the basil leaves and pour into a serving dish, sprinkle with the Parmesan and serve.

Porri al prosciutto
Leeks with ham

2 tablespoons extra virgin olive oil

30g/1 oz butter

100g/3½oz large thick slice of cooked ham, cubed

40g/1½oz raisins, soaked in a little white wine

1.2kg/2lb 10oz leeks, finely sliced

120ml/4fl oz hot vegetable stock

salt and pepper

A simple side dish of leeks that is ideally served with pork dishes and roasts.

Heat the olive oil and butter in a frying pan, add the ham and stir-fry on a medium heat for a couple of minutes.

Stir in the raisins (reserving the wine) and leeks, season with salt and pepper, and stir-fry for a couple of minutes. Add the wine from the raisins and allow to evaporate. Add the vegetable stock, lower the heat, cover with a lid and simmer gently for 15 minutes, until the leeks are soft. Remove from the heat and serve immediately.

Carote brasate al forno
Baked braised carrots with sage and coriander

800g/1lb 12oz carrots, peeled

3 shallots, sliced into segments

1 celery stalk, finely chopped

3 tablespoons extra virgin olive oil

1 teaspoon salt

2 teaspoons coriander powder

3 bay leaves

4 sage leaves

50g/1¾oz butter

250ml/9fl oz vegetable stock, made with the water from the carrots

This is a very nice and different way to cook carrots. Instead of just boiling them without adding any flavouring, here I have parboiled them first, then placed them in the oven with other ingredients to enhance the flavour of the carrots. This makes a perfect accompaniment to main course dishes, especially meat.

Pre-heat the oven to 190°C/375°F/Gas 5.

Parboil the carrots for 15 minutes and drain, reserving the cooking liquid to make the stock.

Put the shallots and celery in an ovenproof dish, and place the carrots on top.

In a bowl combine the olive oil, salt and coriander, and pour this over the carrots. Scatter with the herbs, dot with the butter and pour the vegetable stock over the top.

Cover with foil, place in the oven and bake for 25 minutes until the carrots are tender and cooked through.

Remove from the oven and serve.

Patate al forno con alloro e rosmarino
Roast potatoes with bay leaves and rosemary

6 medium potatoes, all roughly the same size and shape

12 bay leaves

a few sprigs of rosemary

extra virgin olive oil for drizzling

salt and pepper

A simple but very different way of serving roast potatoes. They look and taste lovely!

Pre-heat the oven to 200°C/400°F/Gas 6.

Parboil the unpeeled potatoes in plenty of water for 10 minutes. Drain, cool a little and then peel.

Using a sharp knife, make some slits across the width of each potato but do not cut the whole way through as the potatoes need to stay together. Insert bay leaves in the slits, alternating with rosemary needles.

Place the potatoes in an ovenproof dish or roasting tin, drizzle with olive oil and sprinkle with salt and pepper. Roast in the oven for about 15–20 minutes until golden and cooked through. Serve immediately.

Cipolle al forno
Baked onions

4 medium onions, peeled

3 bay leaves

400ml/14fl oz dry white wine

5 black peppercorns

1 quantity of Basic White Sauce (see page 168)

4 tablespoons extra virgin olive oil

80g/3oz pancetta or bacon, finely chopped

1 small carrot, very finely chopped

1 celery stalk, very finely chopped

30g/1oz Parmesan cheese, freshly grated

pinch of salt

I am surprised that we don't eat more onions whole as a vegetable, but rather we use them as a base in sauces or in salads. This is why I decided to include this recipe. Here the onions are baked whole and served with a delicious white sauce with white wine, vegetables and pancetta. It makes an ideal accompaniment to roast and grilled meats or, of course, is delicious on its own.

Pre-heat the oven to 200°C/400°F/Gas 6.

Parboil the onions with a pinch of salt and 1 bay leaf for 15 minutes.

Meanwhile, put the white wine, peppercorns and the remaining bay leaves in another pan, bring to the boil and allow to evaporate by half. Set aside.

Make the white sauce as per the recipe on page 168.

Heat the olive oil in a pan, add the pancetta or bacon and on a medium heat cook for a couple of minutes. Add the carrot and celery and sweat for about 3 minutes.

In a small ovenproof dish (large enough to accommodate the onions but not too big) scatter half of the pancetta and vegetable mixture on the bottom, followed by the white sauce. Place the onions on top. Top the onions with the rest of the pancetta and vegetable mixture, then sprinkle with the grated Parmesan.

Bake in the oven for 15 minutes until tender and golden.

Remove and serve hot with good bread to dip into the lovely sauce.

Gratinato di patate e formaggio
Cheesy potato bake

1kg/2lb 4oz potatoes, such as King Edward variety

a little butter for greasing

leaves of 1 thyme branch, finely chopped

handful of fresh parsley, finely chopped

200g/7oz fontina or Emmental cheese, grated

100ml/3½fl oz milk

100ml/3½fl oz mascarpone or fresh cream

2 eggs, beaten

a little grated nutmeg

salt and pepper

A lovely, rich potato bake, which makes a perfect side dish or, with all the nutritious ingredients that are included, it can even be a meal in itself. Very simple to make, this is a dish that all the family will love.

Pre-heat the oven to 200°C/400°F/Gas 6.

Peel the potatoes and slice into rounds approximately 3mm thick.

Grease an ovenproof dish with some butter and line it with a layer of potato slices slightly overlapping each other. Sprinkle with some of the herbs, grated cheese and season with salt and pepper. Top with another layer of potato and continue until all your ingredients have finished, keeping aside a handful of cheese.

In a bowl, combine the milk, mascarpone or cream, beaten eggs, a little salt, pepper and the grated nutmeg. Pour this mixture over the layered potatoes, sprinkle with the remaining cheese and bake in the oven for 40 minutes until golden.

Peperonata e riso al forno
Baked pepper stew and rice

350g/12oz long-grain rice, cooked according to the packet instructions

75ml/5 tablespoons extra virgin olive oil

4 anchovy fillets

800g/1lb 12oz mixed peppers, finely sliced into strips

handful of basil leaves

80g/3oz pitted green olives

30g/1oz butter, plus extra for greasing

250g/9oz hard mozzarella, finely chopped

200g/7oz ripe cherry tomatoes, halved and deseeded

salt and pepper

Peperonata is traditionally a dish of peppers that have been stewed with tomatoes. It makes an excellent side dish or can be served with rice. This recipe is slightly different, whereby you cook the peppers without the tomato sauce and add them to cooked rice and cherry tomatoes, and bake it all together.

Pre-heat the oven to 190°C/375°F/Gas 5 and grease an ovenproof dish or roasting tin with a bit of butter.

While the rice is cooking, heat the olive oil in a pan and add the anchovies. Once they have dissolved, stir in the peppers, season with salt and pepper, and add the basil leaves. Cover with a lid and cook on a medium heat for 10 minutes, stirring from time to time.

Drain the cooked rice, stir in the olives, butter and mozzarella, the peppers and cherry tomatoes. Tip into the prepared ovenproof dish and bake in the pre-heated oven for about 10 minutes.

Remove and serve.

kids

When you have children, most people begin to take food seriously and planning nutritious and balanced meals at home becomes a priority. It is so important to instil good, healthy eating habits from an early age, not only for growth and development but also so that in the future they know what good food is and how to eat healthily.

As you probably know, Italians have a lifelong obsession with food – but what you might not know is that they also have an obsession with the wellbeing of their children, almost to the point of madness! From a very early age, babies join in with the family meals – sitting in their highchairs, observing and listening to what is happening at the table. Mothers and grandmothers ensure the babies have a properly balanced meal and they will be encouraged to have three small courses so that all vital nutrients are given. A big fuss is made over the babies if everything is eaten up and, if it is not, the women in the household enter into serious discussions as to what they should give them for the next meal. This attention continues throughout their childhood – and sometimes even into adulthood until the son or daughter leaves home.

Still, I feel we Italians fuss too much over our children's eating habits – as long as the children eat some good food, then it is OK. If they like pasta, give them pasta, varying the sauce if you can. Get them to help with the cooking and encourage them to try new things – if they like, it great; if not, don't worry. I do believe if a child sees you trying new things and eating healthily, then he or she will do so in time, too.

I must admit, it is not easy to feed children, especially when they get to the age where they understand more about the world around them. They can refuse point blank to eat peas or a piece of fish, or suddenly decide they don't like cheese, even though up until the previous day cheese was their favourite food! Children are entitled to change their minds and to have their own likes and dislikes, and sometimes they will simply go through odd phases of refusing certain foods. Believe me – I have two six year olds so I know what it can be like!

I have included a selection of meals here – some pasta, meat, fish and vegetarian – and I hope your children will enjoy them. But they're not just for children – the dishes can be eaten by all the family.

Pasta e piselli
Tubettini with peas

25g/1oz butter

4 tablespoons extra virgin olive oil

1 small onion, finely chopped

2 slices of pancetta or bacon, finely chopped

200g/7oz fresh or frozen peas

4 basil leaves (optional)

1 litre hot water

60g/2oz Parmesan cheese, half shavings and half freshly grated

240g/8½oz tubettini pasta

2 egg yolks

pinch of salt (optional)

This quick and easy pasta dish is a complete meal, which is cooked using only one pan. It is popular throughout Italy and can be made in different ways, using other ingredients such as cream. I find cream a little rich, though, especially for children, so I add egg yolks at the end instead which makes it creamy and more nutritious. It's a great way to get your kids eating eggs if they don't like them – they will never know!

Heat the butter and olive oil in a saucepan, add the onion and pancetta or bacon and stir-fry on a medium heat for a couple of minutes, ensuring they do not burn.

Stir in the peas and basil and cook for a further couple of minutes.

Pour in the water, add a pinch of salt, if using, and the Parmesan shavings, and simmer gently for 10 minutes in order for the flavours to infuse.

Add the pasta and cook with the lid half on until *al dente*, stirring from time to time. Add more hot water, if necessary. The pasta needs to be able to cook properly but once it is *al dente*, the water should have been absorbed.

Meanwhile, beat the egg yolks and grated Parmesan in a small bowl. Add this to the pasta and mix well until cooked.

Remove from the heat and serve immediately.

Tip: *You can add a few cherry tomatoes with the pasta to give the dish a little colour.*

Pastina in brodo
Little pasta shapes in broth

approx. 1 litre/1¾ pints Vegetable Broth or Beef Broth (see pages 34 and 41)

200g/7oz pastina

some Parmesan cheese, freshly grated, to serve

This is the perfect Italian comfort food. All generations love it and in most Italian homes it is served in the evening as a first course, since it is light and nutritious. There is nothing more warming and homely than a broth and is the ideal weaning food for babies. Try to get the small pasta shapes, such as alphabet, stars, tiny shells, sementi (like tiny seeds) or any others you find or your child likes. I dedicate this recipe to my daughters, Dominique, Chloe and Olivia, and my grandsons, Eoin and Dylan, who absolutely adore it.

Sieve the broth into a saucepan, bring to the boil, add the pastina and simmer gently until they are *al dente*.

Serve hot with some grated Parmesan.

Tip: Adjust the amount of broth depending on whether you like it soupy or thick.

Uova in trippa
Eggy strips in tomato sauce

400g/14oz tomato passata

1 tablespoon finely chopped onion

100g/3½oz fresh or frozen peas

a few basil leaves

2 tablespoons extra virgin olive oil

4 eggs

knob of butter

some Parmesan cheese, freshly grated, to serve

salt (optional)

The Italian title suggests this is a tripe dish but, fear not, it is only called this because the strips of egg with tomato sauce resemble tripe! This is a fun way of eating an omelette and is often made for children in Italy. As a child I remember eating this dish when it had been made using our own fresh eggs and our own homemade passata. It is very simple to prepare and is a quick, nutritious meal for children and their parents.

In a saucepan over a high heat, place the tomato passata, onion, peas, basil leaves, olive oil and a pinch of salt, if using. Stir and bring to the boil. Reduce the heat, cover with a lid and simmer gently for about 15 minutes, stirring from time to time.

Meanwhile, beat the eggs together with some salt, if using.

Heat the butter in a small frying pan and add half of the beaten eggs. Fry on both sides like an omelette over a medium heat, remove and do the same with the rest of the egg. Leave the omelettes to cool slightly, then slice into strips about 1cm wide.

Add the strips to the hot tomato sauce, take off the heat and serve with some grated Parmesan.

Tip: To make the dish richer, you can add some finely chopped cheese and ham to the egg mixture.

Risotto alle fragole
Strawberry risotto

4 tablespoons extra virgin olive oil

2 small shallots, finely chopped

250g/9oz Arborio rice

1 litre/1¾ pints vegetable stock, kept hot

500g/1lb 2oz strawberries, hulled – half quartered and half roughly chopped

40g/1½oz butter

70g/2½oz Parmesan cheese

salt (optional)

This risotto used to be fashionable during the 70s and 80s in Italy, and is now making a comeback, as Italians rediscover that fruit can be just as delicious in main courses. I made this for the family last summer – the fridge was bare and all we had were some punnets of strawberries and risotto rice in the cupboard. Instead of the usual plain risotto, I livened it up with the strawberries. The girls loved it and were fascinated by the fact that you could have a risotto with strawberries in it! It is an ideal dish for the English strawberry season when they are in abundance and is a good way of adding more fruit to your child's diet. Strawberries are packed full of goodness and are a great source of vitamin C.

Heat the olive oil in a saucepan, add the shallots and allow to sweat over a medium heat.

Stir in the rice and make sure each grain is coated with oil.

Add a ladleful of hot stock, stir and simmer for a minute, until absorbed.

Stir in the roughly chopped strawberries and then gradually add the remaining stock as you would in the Basic Risotto recipe (see page 76).

When the rice is *al dente*, remove from the heat and stir in the butter and half of the grated Parmesan, and season with salt, if using.

Leave to rest for a minute, then top with the quartered strawberries and remaining grated Parmesan, and serve.

Pasta e patate
Pasta and potatoes

4 tablespoons extra virgin olive oil

1 medium onion, very finely chopped

1 carrot, finely chopped

2 slices pancetta or bacon, very finely chopped

600g/1lb 5oz potatoes, peeled and cubed

handful of celery leaves, finely chopped

6 cherry tomatoes (optional)

1.2 litres/2 pints boiling water

250g/9oz macaroni

40g/1½oz Parmesan cheese, freshly grated

salt and pepper (optional)

This is a traditional southern Italian recipe, and can be made with rice instead of pasta. It is comfort food at its best and was one of my favourite childhood meals – and still is today! There are many versions of this dish, but this one is the most nutritious and the simplest – it is all cooked quickly and easily in one saucepan.

Heat the olive oil in a saucepan, add the onion, carrot and pancetta or bacon, and stir-fry for a couple of minutes over a high heat.

Then add the potatoes, celery leaves and tomatoes, if using. Stir well, reduce the heat to medium and cook for 4 minutes, mixing with a wooden spoon to avoid sticking and burning.

Pour in the water, sprinkle with some salt, if using, and leave to simmer gently until the potatoes are tender.

Use a masher to squash the potatoes slightly, but do not mash. Add the pasta and cook until *al dente*, stirring from time to time.

Remove from the heat and mix in the grated Parmesan. Leave to rest for a minute, then serve.

Fritelle di patate
Potato cakes with leeks and bacon

600g/1lb 5oz potatoes, peeled and roughly chopped

4 tablespoons extra virgin olive oil

1 leek, finely chopped

50g/1¾oz bacon, finely chopped

2 egg yolks

10g/¼oz Parmesan cheese, freshly grated

60g/2¼oz plain flour

salt (optional)

These are tasty and nutritious savoury treats that your children will love. They take very little time to prepare and cook, and make a nice snack or accompaniment to a meal. They can be dipped in Tomato Sauce (see page 165) – my version of ketchup! Delicious for adults, too – I would serve the potato cakes with a green leaf salad dressed with extra virgin olive oil and balsamic vinegar.

Boil the potatoes in plenty of slightly salted water until tender. Drain and mash.

Put 1 tablespoon of olive oil in a pan, add the leek and bacon, and sauté over a medium heat, stirring from time to time to ensure it doesn't burn.

Add the eggs yolks, Parmesan, flour and a pinch of salt, if using, to the mash. Then add the leek and bacon, and mix well. With your hands, take a little of the mixture and form flat rounds.

Heat the remaining olive oil in a large frying pan. Cook the potato cakes over a medium heat on both sides until golden.

Remove, drain on kitchen paper and serve.

Petti di pollo farciti
Filled chicken breasts

4 large slices of chicken breast, approx. 100g/3½oz each

100g/3½oz ricotta

a few marjoram leaves, finely chopped

4 slices of cooked ham, slightly smaller than the chicken slices

plain flour for dusting

30g/1oz butter

2 tablespoons extra virgin olive oil

200ml/7fl oz hot chicken stock

salt (optional)

There are so many ready-made varieties of stuffed chicken breast on the market, but most are, quite frankly, awful. Try making your own – they will surely taste better and you'll know what goes into them. Children generally like chicken and the filling makes the meat nice and moist, and really yummy.

Put the chicken slices between 2 sheets of cling film and pound with a meat mallet to get them really thin.

Combine the ricotta, marjoram and some salt, if using.

Arrange the slices of chicken on a work surface and top with the ham, ensuring there is a border around the edge.

Place a dollop of the ricotta mixture in the middle of each one. Fold the slices in half, pressing down on the edges gently, making sure the filling does not escape. Dust with flour.

Put the butter and olive oil in a large frying pan over a high heat, add the filled chicken pieces and seal on both sides.

Reduce the heat, add the hot stock and simmer gently for about 5 minutes until the chicken has cooked through.

Remove from the heat and serve with a little of the cooking juices, if desired.

Polpettine di pesce
Fishballs

4 tablespoons extra virgin olive oil

1 garlic clove, squashed and left whole

1 medium onion, finely chopped

500g/1lb 2oz cod fillet, lightly steamed and flaked

2 eggs

4 tablespoons breadcrumbs

3 tablespoons milk

40g/1½oz Parmesan cheese, freshly grated

plain flour for dusting

oil for frying and greasing

salt and freshly ground black pepper (optional)

These delicious fishballs will surely appeal to children. Although lightly fried, they are then baked in the oven, making them healthy and nutritious. Serve with a fresh and tangy Basil and Lemon Sauce (see page 173) for a truly delicious feast.

Heat the olive oil in a pan and sweat the garlic and onion over a medium heat for about 4 minutes. Leave to cool, then discard the garlic.

In a bowl, combine the cod with the onion, eggs, breadcrumbs, milk and Parmesan, and season with salt and pepper, if using. Mix well and place in the fridge for about 10 minutes to firm.

Meanwhile, pre-heat the oven to 180°C/350°F/Gas 4 and lightly grease a baking tray with some olive oil. Set aside.

Remove the fish mixture from the fridge and form into balls roughly the size of golf balls, pressing them slightly. Dust with some plain flour.

Heat the frying oil in a large pan and, when hot, add the fishballs and fry for a couple of minutes on each side.

Remove and place on the baking tray. Bake in the pre-heated oven for about 15 minutes until golden.

Remove and serve with Basil and Lemon Sauce (see page 173).

Salsicce e patate
Baked sausages and potatoes

6 medium potatoes, peeled and cut into bite-sized chunks

3 bay leaves

4 tablespoons extra virgin olive oil

8 good-quality pork sausages

pinch of salt (optional)

Most children like sausages and baking is a much healthier way of cooking them than frying, and the addition of potatoes makes this dish a complete meal. Easy, quick and economical – what more can I say?

Pre-heat the oven to 200°C/400°F/Gas 6.

Place the potato chunks in a bowl and mix well with some salt, if using, bay leaves and the olive oil.

Place the sausages in a roasting tin or ovenproof dish. Prick all over with a fork. Arrange the potatoes around them, cover with foil and bake in the oven for 15 minutes.

Remove the foil and continue to bake for a further 25 minutes, turning occasionally, until the sausages and potatoes are cooked.

Remove from the oven and serve.

Muffin al mais
Savoury sweetcorn muffins

2 eggs, beaten

85ml/3fl oz milk

110g/4oz butter, melted

250g/9oz plain flour

2 teaspoons baking powder

½ teaspoon bicarbonate of soda

100g/3½oz tinned sweetcorn, drained

30g/1oz cooked ham, finely chopped

30g/1oz Parmesan cheese, freshly grated

pinch of salt (optional)

8 muffin paper cases

Muffins are fashionable now in Italy, so I decided to include a savoury muffin recipe for the children's section. They are a great teatime snack and, because they are homemade, you know you will be giving your children the best. If you prefer, you can substitute peas for the sweetcorn and omit the ham or replace it with salami. I dedicate this recipe to my nephew, Mario, who is a muffin maniac!

Pre-heat the oven to 180°C/350°F/Gas 4.

In a bowl, combine the eggs, milk and melted butter.

Gently fold in the flour, baking powder, bicarbonate of soda and salt, if using. Then stir in the sweetcorn, ham and Parmesan.

Divide between the 8 paper cases and fill to the top without levelling out.

Bake in the oven for 30 minutes until golden. You can check if they are ready by inserting a wooden skewer – if it comes out dry, the muffins are done.

Leave to cool and enjoy!

sauces

This might be the smallest chapter in the book, but it is certainly one of the most important. Sauces form the basis of many dishes, like the Bolognese ragout and white sauce that combine to make delicious lasagne. Other sauces make wonderful accompaniments, such as the Salsa Verde (see page 175–6) which is particularly good served alongside boiled or cold meats, Balsamic Red Onion Relish (see page 174) which goes really well with cheese, or the Basil and Lemon Sauce (see page 173) which is a must for fish.

In Italian cooking, there are lots of sauces for dressing pasta and some are essential in every Italian kitchen. I like to make a huge pot of tomato sauce and store it in batches in the freezer, so that we always have some at home – for quick meals, unexpected guests or for using in other recipes. When you make a classic sauce, such as tomato, Bolognese or pesto, it is always worth making extra to freeze and use later. This is also true when you find bargains at your local market. If, for example, aubergines or peppers are in season, make a large pot of sauce with these ingredients (see page 169) and freeze for another day. The best fast food you could ever wish for – just defrost your sauce, heat it through and cook some pasta to go with it. Quicker than waiting for a takeaway and much more nutritious, delicious and economical, too!

Pesto
Fresh basil sauce

80g/3oz fresh basil

2 tablespoons pine kernels

1 garlic clove

½ teaspoon coarse sea salt

200ml/7fl oz extra virgin olive oil

2 tablespoons pecorino cheese, freshly grated

This is a traditional sauce from Liguria, where lovely, sweet basil grows in abundance and delicate extra virgin olive oil is produced. You can find ready-made pesto everywhere these days but it's really nice to make your own. Traditionally the sauce was made using a pestle and mortar but you can use a food processor. Fresh pesto keeps in the fridge for about a week but you can also freeze it for later use. If you keep it in the fridge, make sure you add some extra virgin olive oil over the top to preserve it. When you use the preserved pesto, add a little hot water in order to return it to a smooth paste.

First of all, remove and discard the stalks from the basil, and keep the leaves to one side.

Place the pine kernels, garlic and sea salt in a mortar and grind with a pestle. Add a few basil leaves and some olive oil and grind and stir with the pestle.

Continue this procedure until you have used up all the basil leaves and about 100ml of the olive oil. The sauce should have a smooth, silky consistency.

Finally, add the remaining olive oil and the pecorino cheese and mix well.

Tip: If you want to make the pesto in a food processor, place all the ingredients inside and whiz until you obtain a smooth paste.

Salsa al burro e salvia
Butter and sage sauce

100g/3½oz butter

4 sage leaves

2 tablespoons cooking water

4 tablespoons Parmesan cheese, freshly grated

This is the world's quickest sauce – Italian fast food at its best! In fact, I dedicate this recipe to my daughter Olivia who would live on pasta with butter if she could. This sauce is perfect for dressing pasta, gnocchi or even boiled rice.

Place the butter with the sage leaves in a large frying pan, and cook on a gentle heat until the butter begins to bubble. At this stage, quickly drain the pasta/gnocchi/rice, reserving two tablespoons of the cooking water to give the sauce a little more moisture.

Add the pasta/gnocchi/rice to the frying pan together with the reserved cooking water and mix well.

Stir in the Parmesan and serve immediately.

Salsa di pomodoro
Tomato sauce

4 tablespoons olive oil

2 garlic cloves, finely chopped, or ½ medium onion, finely chopped

2 x 410g tins plum tomatoes, chopped

handful of fresh basil, finely chopped

salt and pepper

This is the most basic Italian tomato sauce and is the most widely used to flavour pasta and other dishes. It's always handy to make a large quantity and freeze it in batches for use at other times. I have given you an option of either garlic or onion – this is because a certain dish will sometimes require one or the other. For example, the tomato sauce with garlic goes well with fish and seafood dishes, while the tomato sauce with onion goes better with meat-based dishes and food that requires a lighter-tasting tomato sauce.

Heat the olive oil in a large frying pan and sweat the garlic or onion over a medium heat.

Add the tomatoes and basil, season with salt and pepper, and simmer for 25 minutes.

Remove from the heat and use immediately, or leave to cool and place in the fridge or freezer for later use.

Pesto alle mandorle
Almond pesto sauce

4 ripe vine tomatoes, deseeded and roughly chopped

6 large basil leaves

4 mint leaves

50g/1¾oz flaked almonds

10 green olives, pitted

1 tablespoon capers

zest of ¼ of an orange

2 tablespoons pecorino cheese, freshly grated

100ml/8 tablespoons extra virgin olive oil

This is a Sicilian pesto that uses a variety of ingredients, mainly almonds, and is delicately flavoured with orange zest. Ideal for those who prefer a more subtle taste than the pungent basil of traditional pesto. Perfect for dressing pasta and for topping crostini.

Place all the ingredients in a food processor and whiz until you obtain a smooth paste.

Salsa bianca base
Basic white sauce

50g/1¾oz butter

50g/1¾oz plain flour

500ml/18fl oz hot milk

salt and freshly ground black pepper, or a pinch of grated nutmeg

I often hear complaints from people that they cannot make a white sauce and so they end up buying a ready-made version. If you follow a few simple rules, it really is easy and it makes such a difference to have a homemade sauce in dishes such as lasagne, baked pasta or gnocchi. Firstly, make sure you have all your ingredients ready before starting and ensure the milk is hot. Cook it on a low heat to avoid burning and use the correct amount of butter and flour otherwise you'll end up with lumps. Finally, always use a wooden spoon or, better still, a small hand whisk and keep stirring! I usually flavour my white sauce with grated cheese such as Parmesan, or whatever the recipe suggests. Good luck and Buon Appetito!

Melt the butter in a small pan over a low heat.

Once melted, add the flour, mixing well to obtain a smooth paste, stirring all the time.

Gradually add the hot milk, stirring constantly, until the sauce begins to thicken.

After about 10 minutes, when the sauce has thickened, remove from the heat and season with salt and pepper or nutmeg.

Tip: If you find that the sauce gets lumpy, use a small hand whisk and stir until the lumps disappear.

Sugo alle melanzane
Aubergine sauce

180ml/6fl oz oil for frying

400g/14oz aubergines, cut into cubes

4 tablespoons extra virgin olive oil

1 garlic clove

400g/14oz tinned plum tomatoes, chopped

handful of fresh basil, finely chopped

salt and pepper

This is ideal for dressing spaghetti, fusilli or penne pasta, as well as for serving as an accompaniment to meat dishes and even for using as a filling for panini. You can also make a pepper sauce by following the same recipe, substituting red and yellow peppers for the aubergines.

Heat the oil in a large frying pan and cook the aubergine cubes until golden. Remove, drain and place on kitchen paper.

Meanwhile, heat the olive oil in a pan, add the garlic and sauté over a medium heat. Add the tomatoes and cook for 10 minutes.

Add the fried aubergine cubes and basil, season with a pinch of salt and pepper, and continue to cook for a further couple of minutes.

Remove from the heat and use accordingly.

Salsa agrodolce
Italian sweet and sour sauce

3 tablespoons extra virgin olive oil

1 carrot, grated

1 medium onion, very finely chopped

1 stick of celery, very finely chopped

560g/1lb 4oz passata

leaves of 1 thyme branch

1 teaspoon sugar

2 tablespoons white wine vinegar

salt and pepper

This tomato-based sauce is quick and easy to prepare and is ideal for dressing short pasta, rice and breadcrumbed meat cutlets. It has a lovely tangy taste and it is worth making more to freeze.

Heat the olive oil in a pan, add the carrot, onion and celery, and sweat over a medium heat.

Add the passata, thyme and sugar, partially cover with a lid and cook for 25 minutes, stirring from time to time.

Add the vinegar, season with salt and pepper, and mix well.

Remove from the heat and use or store accordingly.

Salsa al basilico per pesce
Basil and lemon sauce

150ml/5fl oz vegetable stock

150ml/5fl oz white wine

3 shallots, roughly chopped

1 medium potato, finely chopped

handful of basil leaves, roughly torn

1 tablespoon extra virgin olive oil

juice of ½ lemon

1 teaspoon lemon zest

salt and pepper

This simple, delicate sauce is a must for fish. It will liven up plain steamed fish such as cod, hake, halibut or plaice, and is also ideal with Fishballs (see page 152).

Bring the stock and wine to the boil in a small pan, add the shallots and potato and simmer on a gentle heat until tender.

Remove from the heat and place in a bowl together with the basil and olive oil. Use a hand blender to combine all the ingredients together, until you obtain a smooth consistency.

Stir in the lemon juice, lemon zest, season with salt and pepper, and serve.

Composta di cipolle rosse al balsamico
Balsamic red onion relish

300g/10½oz red onions, well peeled and finely sliced

150g/5½oz granulated sugar

1 tablespoon runny honey

balsamic vinegar for drizzling

I love chutneys and relishes but find the bought ones full of unnecessary ingredients and additives. This is my version of a simple homemade onion relish using the minimum of ingredients. It can be enjoyed with cheese, and boiled, grilled or roasted meats. It is worth increasing the quantities and making a large batch to keep. If you do this, remember to sterilize your jars and it will keep for a couple of months. Once opened, store in the fridge.

Place the onions, sugar and honey in a saucepan over a medium heat. Cook for about 40 minutes, stirring quite often, until you obtain a dense consistency.

Remove from the heat, drizzle with some balsamic vinegar, allow to cool and serve or store accordingly.

Salsa verde
Parsley and caper sauce

80g/3oz parsley, finely chopped

50g/1¾oz capers, finely chopped

1 garlic clove, finely chopped

1 anchovy, finely chopped

3 cocktail gherkins, finely chopped

1 egg yolk, hard-boiled

75ml/5 tablespoons extra virgin olive oil

1 tablespoon white wine vinegar

salt and pepper

Salsa verde literally translated means 'green sauce' and it is called this for obvious reasons. It is widely used throughout Italy to flavour meat and fish dishes. I usually chop everything with a mezzaluna or very sharp knife as I prefer the crunchy texture of the ingredients, but if you like you can use a food processor. The sauce can be stored in the fridge for up to a week.

Combine all the finely chopped ingredients in a bowl. Crumble in the egg yolk, add the olive oil and vinegar, season with salt and pepper, and carefully stir well. Leave to rest for a few minutes before using.

Desserts

Traditionally, the dessert course was simply some fruit of the season. Fruit is probably all you want to eat after a first course of pasta or risotto followed by meat or fish and vegetables! On Sundays and other feast days, though, desserts would be served. I remember in our house we would normally have a crostata di frutta o marmellata (a fruit or jam tart), which my mother made using up leftover fruit or homemade jam.

These days, it is still seasonal fruit and sometimes yoghurts that are served, but elaborate desserts are also becoming more and more common. Most of the desserts that I enjoy contain fruit – it is a good way of using up abundant seasonal fruit, as well as making the dessert healthier.

When I was growing up in Italy, I had never heard of the now-popular tiramisu, and it is only since living in England that I've noticed this dessert appear in all Italian restaurants and become a classic. The main ingredient is mascarpone cheese, which is now widely available in England and can be used in many other desserts, too.

When I was a young boy, I had never tasted cream and I suppose this is one reason why I use it so very, very rarely in my recipes. The nearest I got to it was freshly made ricotta given to us by local farmers – now that was a real treat! Ricotta is widely used in desserts in southern Italy and it is one of the main ingredients in a whole number of cakes and tarts, and in the Sicilian sweet treats, such as cannoli and cassata. For a really quick dessert try Ricotta Pudding (see page 202) – I've suggested a few different great ways of serving this wonderful ingredient.

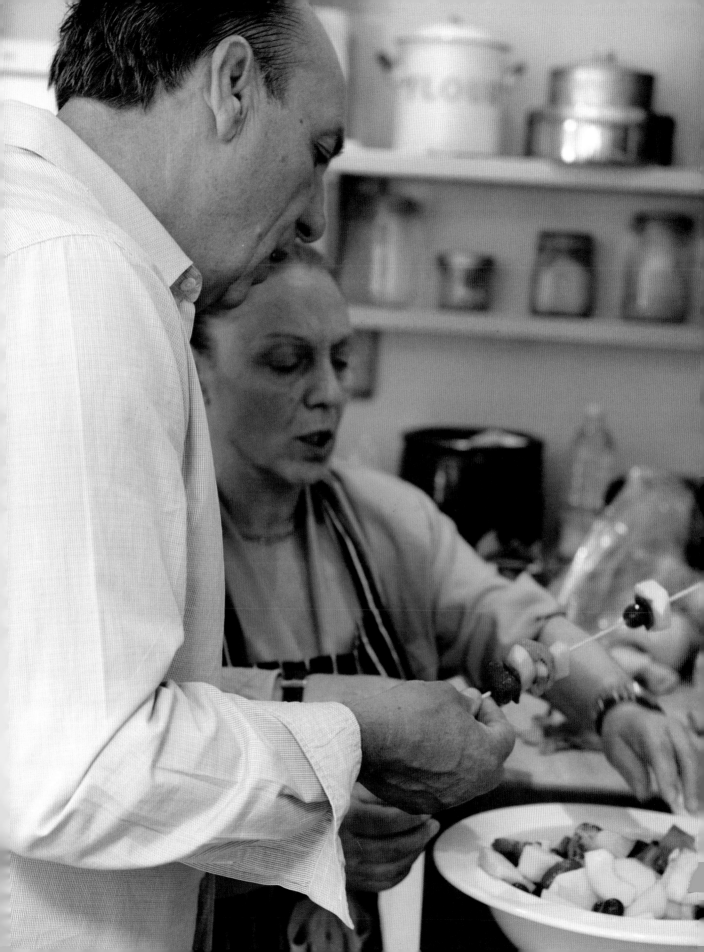

Fragole al basilico di Chloe
Chloe's strawberry and basil salad

500g/1 lb 2oz strawberries, hulled and quartered

50g/1¾oz caster sugar

juice and zest of 1 orange

10 basil leaves

This is my daughter Chloe's recipe. She created it while Liz was cooking for some guests one day – she just picked these ingredients and put them together. Liz was about to throw it away, when she saw that, in fact, it looked quite edible and smelt rather nice. She tried it and it was, indeed, really good. It's a very easy dessert to make, and would be especially good when the lovely sweet English strawberries are in season. Well done, Chloe!

Place the strawberries with the sugar, orange juice and zest, and 6 of the basil leaves. Leave to macerate for about 30 minutes in the fridge.

Remove from the fridge, divide between 4 bowls or glasses, decorate with the remaining basil leaves and serve.

Gelato all'amaretto con salsa di fragole
Amaretto ice cream with strawberry sauce

400g/14oz vanilla ice cream

100g/3½oz amaretti biscuits, crushed

2 tablespoons Port, vin santo, Marsala or any sweet wine

170ml/6fl oz double cream, whisked until firm (optional)

biscuits, to serve (optional)

for the strawberry sauce

200g/7oz strawberries, hulled and roughly chopped

10g/¼oz caster sugar

3 tablespoons Port, vin santo, Marsala or any sweet wine

Transform vanilla ice cream into amaretto ice cream quickly and easily! Serve with a hot strawberry sauce for a lovely dessert. You may also add double cream, if you wish.

Bring the vanilla ice cream to room temperature, then stir in the crushed amaretti biscuits and sweet wine. Return to the freezer for about 15 minutes.

Meanwhile, make the strawberry sauce by placing all the ingredients in a small pan over a medium heat and cook for about 15 minutes, stirring all the time, until you obtain a smooth creamy consistency.

Remove the ice cream from the freezer. Divide between 4 small bowls or glasses, top with piped double cream (if using) and pour over the hot strawberry sauce. Serve immediately with biscuits, if desired.

Crostata di rabarbaro e fragole
Rhubarb and strawberry tart

700g/1lb 9oz rhubarb, cleaned and trimmed

200g/7oz caster sugar

300g/10½oz fresh strawberries, hulled, sliced in half (if they are not in season, use frozen strawberries instead, and defrost and use as below)

1 egg, beaten

sifted icing sugar to sprinkle

for the pastry

175g/6oz plain flour, sifted

75g/2¾oz unsalted butter, plus extra for greasing

75g/2¾oz sugar

zest of ½ lemon

2 egg yolks

Rhubarb always makes me think of England and its delicious desserts. Although you can find rhubarb in Italy, it is mainly used in liqueurs and boiled sweets. I wanted to put a classic crostata (tart) in this book but was stuck for a filling – that is until I saw some lovely rhubarb at my local market! I have combined the classic Italian crostata with a very English filling. The added strawberries give sweetness to the rhubarb.

Pre-heat the oven to 180°C/350°F/Gas 4 and grease a 20cm/8in tart tin with butter.

To make the pastry, place the flour in a bowl or on a clean work surface, and rub in the butter until it resembles breadcrumbs. Add the sugar, lemon zest and egg yolks, mixing well until you obtain a smooth pastry.

Roll the pastry out to a thickness of about 5mm and line the greased tart tin with it, reserving the trimmings. Form the trimmings back into a ball and store in the fridge.

Bake the tart blind for 25 minutes.

Meanwhile, place the rhubarb and sugar in a saucepan over a gentle heat and cook for about 5–7 minutes until the rhubarb is soft but still has some texture.

Remove and strain the rhubarb very thoroughly, reserving the juice, if desired. Allow to cool, then stir the strawberries into the rhubarb.

Remove the pastry case from the oven and fill with the rhubarb and strawberry filling.

Roll out the reserved pastry trimmings and cut out strips. Place them criss-crossed over the top of the tart in a lattice pattern. Brush the strips with the beaten egg and return the tart to the oven for a further 10 minutes, until the strips are lightly golden.

Remove, leave to cool slightly, sprinkle with icing sugar and serve with some cream or custard, if desired – otherwise, it is delicious on its own.

Tip: *You can either drink the reserved rhubarb liquid or make a sauce by thickening it with a little cornflour. Delicious served hot with the tart.*

Mele meringate
Apple meringue

4 apples, peeled, cored, cut into segments and blanched for 2 minutes

50g/1¾oz sugar

16 Savoiardi biscuits (see page 218) or sponge fingers

100ml/3½fl oz apple juice

for the cream

4 egg yolks

150g/5½oz sugar

40g/1½oz plain flour

500ml/18fl oz hot milk

grated zest of 1 lemon

for the meringue

100g/3½oz egg white

100g/3½oz sugar

pinch of salt

Meringue desserts are becoming ever-more popular in Italy and this is so simple to make and delicious to eat, it's easy to see why.

First make the cream by beating the egg yolks and sugar. Stir in the flour. Gradually add the hot milk, whisking all the time to avoid lumps forming. Place over a low heat and allow to bubble gently for about 10 minutes, stirring all the time. Remove from the heat, add the lemon zest and set aside.

Place the apple segments in a pan with the sugar, put over a medium heat and gently cook until the apples caramelize. Remove from the heat and set aside.

Meanwhile, make the meringue by whisking the egg whites, sugar and pinch of salt. When they are stiff, put to one side.

Place the biscuits along the bottom of an ovenproof dish and drizzle a little apple juice over the top. Pour on the cream and top with the apple segments. Place the meringue in a piping bag with a decorative nozzle and pipe swirls next to each apple slice, or cover entirely with the meringue.

Finally, place under a hot grill for a few minutes until the meringue is golden. Remove and serve hot or cold.

Spiedini di frutta
Mixed fruit skewers with a minty mascarpone dip

200g/7oz strawberries, hulled and halved

½ melon, cut into chunks

2 apples, cored and cut into chunks

2 peaches, if in season, stoned and cut into chunks

2 kiwi fruit, peeled and cut into chunks

a couple of slices of pineapple, cut into chunks

handful of black grapes, left whole

50g/1¾oz soft brown sugar

juice of 1 orange

250g/9 oz mascarpone

2 tablespoons runny honey

roughly 12 mint leaves, finely chopped – add more mint if you like a more minty taste

Lovely to look at, delicious to eat and easy to prepare, these fruit skewers can be served as an impressive dessert, as a healthy, kick-start breakfast or as a snack at any time of day. It is ideal if you have lots of fruit in the house and you can be flexible with the type of fruit you use. Make the most of whatever is in season. The addition of the mascarpone dip makes this a complete dessert and great for when you have guests.

Put all the fruit in a bowl together with the sugar and orange juice. Place in the fridge and leave to macerate for about 15 minutes.

Remove from the fridge and place on skewers, alternating the fruit.

Mix the mascarpone and honey with the mint leaves and serve with the fruit skewers.

Carpaccio di nettarine ubriache
Carpaccio of nectarine

2 nectarines, washed and pitted, sliced very thinly

1 tablespoon raisins

150ml/5fl oz vin santo or a sweet white wine

8 small crunchy amaretti biscuits

a few mint leaves

This is a really quick and simple dessert, which is delicious, too! The secret is to find really good nectarines so only buy them when they are in season during the summer. You'll need ripe but firm fruit in order to get the lovely sweet taste but still be able to slice it thinly. A perfect, light summer dish.

Place the nectarine slices and raisins in a bowl with the vin santo or sweet white wine and leave to marinate for 30 minutes.

Remove the nectarine slices and arrange on a serving dish or divide between 4 individual bowls.

Place the marinade juices with the raisins in a small pan, put on a medium heat and reduce by about half. Leave to cool.

Meanwhile, top the fruit with the crushed amaretti and mint leaves. Pour over the marinade and serve.

Tiramisu al limone
Lemon tiramisu pudding

2 egg yolks

75g/2¾oz caster sugar

150g/5½oz mascarpone

2 tablespoons limoncello (lemon liqueur)

1 teaspoon grated lemon zest

2 egg whites, whisked until stiff and forming peaks

20 sponge biscuits

for the lemon essence

15g/½oz lemon peel, pith removed

20g/¾oz sugar

100ml/3½fl oz water

This is a deliciously light tiramisu, which is quite common where I come from because of the lovely lemons that the Amalfi coast is so famous for. Make sure you get good unwaxed lemons. I dedicate this recipe to my nephew, Francesco, who used to make it when he worked in one of the local restaurants at home.

Beat the egg yolks and sugar until creamy and fluffy. Stir in the mascarpone and continue to beat with a whisk. Add the limoncello and lemon zest and stir. Fold in the stiff egg whites until well amalgamated. Set aside.

In a pan on a medium heat, place all the ingredients for the lemon essence. Allow to simmer for 3–4 minutes until the sugar has dissolved and the liquid has reduced slightly. Remove from the heat and leave to cool. Take out the lemon peel, finely chop and set aside.

Line a serving dish with some of the mascarpone cream followed by a layer of biscuits which have been dipped in the lemon essence. Top with some more mascarpone and continue with these layers until the ingredients have finished, being sure to end with a layer of mascarpone cream.

Top with the finely chopped lemon peel and leave in the fridge until required.

Tip: This can be eaten as soon as it's made but improves if it's left in the fridge for a couple of hours. It can even be made the day before you need it.

Pere al forno con vin santo e mascarpone
Baked pears with vin santo and mascarpone

4 ripe conference pears

150ml/5fl oz vin santo

150ml/5fl oz water

50g/1¾oz caster sugar

200g/7oz mascarpone

1 vanilla pod, split and seeds removed

The combination of cooked pears and mascarpone is delicious and the additional sauce makes this an even lovelier, sophistic-ated dessert. It is a must for a Sunday lunch or when you have guests. I have used vin santo to make the sauce, but Marsala or Port are equally good.

Pre-heat the oven to 200°C/400°F/Gas 6.

Cut the pears in half and scoop out the core. Place them in a saucepan skin side down with the vin santo, water and sugar. Bring to the boil, reduce the heat to medium, cover with a lid and cook for 10–15 minutes, until the pears are soft but not mushy.

Carefully remove the pears and leave to cool slightly, reserving the cooking liquid.

Scoop out a little of the pulp and roughly chop. Combine this with the mascarpone and vanilla pod seeds. Place a little of this mixture into the cavity of each pear half.

Pour half of the cooking liquid into an ovenproof dish. Add the pear halves and place in the oven for about 10 minutes, until they are heated through.

Gently heat the remaining liquid and simmer until it evaporates and thickens slightly – not too much or you'll end up with a thick, sticky caramel.

Remove the pears from the oven, place on a serving dish, pour over the sauce and serve immediately.

Ravioli di fichi e noci
Italian mince pies

160g/5¾oz dried figs, finely chopped

40g/1½oz walnuts, finely chopped

2 tablespoons pine nuts

1 teaspoon fennel seeds (optional)

pinch of cinnamon

grated zest of ½ lemon

grated zest of ½ orange

50ml/2fl oz Marsala, vin santo or amaretto liqueur

1 tablespoon water

1 egg, beaten

icing sugar for dusting

for the pastry

175g/6oz plain flour

75g/2¾oz unsalted butter

75g/2¾oz caster sugar

2 egg yolks

These are mince pies with an Italian touch! They are much less sweet than the English variety (although I do love the English ones if they are homemade) and are something a little different for the festive season – or any time of year. The word 'ravioli' in the Italian title suggests they should be made with a ravioli cutter and then fried but I leave it to you. I have used a plain round cutter and baked them as you would English mince pies. If you don't have time to make your own pastry, use 350g/12oz ready-made, sweet shortcrust pastry instead.

Place the flour and butter in a large bowl or on a clean work surface. Rub the butter into the flour until it resembles breadcrumbs. Stir in the sugar, then add the egg yolks and mix until you obtain a smooth, soft pastry. Form into a ball, wrap in cling film and place in the fridge while you make the filling.

Pre-heat the oven to 180°C/350°F/Gas 4.

Combine all the remaining ingredients in a bowl, except the beaten egg and icing sugar, and mix well. Put to one side until needed.

Roll the pastry out on a floured work surface, to a thickness of about 3mm/⅛in. Cut rounds of about 7cm/2¾in diameter with a pastry cutter. Place a little of the filling in the centre of half of the rounds.

Brush the edges of the rounds with beaten egg and place the unfilled rounds over the top of the filled rounds and press down well at the edges so the filling cannot escape.

Place the pies on a baking tray and bake for about 15–20 minutes until golden brown. Remove from the oven and dust with icing sugar.

Budino al cioccolato e amaretto
Chocolate and amaretto pudding

50g/1¾oz plain flour

50g/1¾oz sugar

500ml/18fl oz hot milk

100g/3½oz dark chocolate, finely chopped

1 vanilla pod, split

80ml/2½fl oz amaretto liqueur

50g/1¾oz butter

60g/2¼oz small amaretti biscuits for garnish

A simple, old-fashioned chocolate pudding that is not too sweet and is very easy to prepare. The amaretto liqueur gives the dish a bit of a kick – but not too much!

Combine the flour and sugar in a saucepan, and gradually add the hot milk, whisking all the time to prevent lumps forming.

Stir in the chocolate, vanilla and amaretto liqueur. Mix well.

Place over a medium heat and cook for about 2 minutes, stirring with a wooden spoon. Add the butter and continue to stir on the heat for a further 2 minutes, until it begins to thicken.

Remove from the heat and discard the vanilla pod.

Prepare a small pudding basin or 4 individual ones by wetting them slightly before pouring the mixture in (this prevents sticking), or line with cling film. Leave to cool, then place in the fridge to set.

Crush a few of the small amaretti biscuits and scatter over the pudding. Garnish with the remaining biscuits and serve.

Ricotta dolce
Ricotta pudding

400g/14oz ricotta

150g/5½oz caster sugar

seeds of 1 vanilla pod

150g/5½oz double cream,
whipped until stiff

Ricotta cheese is widely used in Italy in desserts and cakes. It is ideal as it is light and not high in fat and calories, and it is even given to babies in Italy! As a child, I remember eating freshly made ricotta while it was still warm, mixed with a little sugar, and it was always a most welcome and yummy pudding. As well as the basic recipe, here are a few ideas on how to make this versatile cheese into other quick desserts. You could add a little liqueur to any of these recipes, if you wish.

Combine the ricotta, sugar and vanilla seeds with a whisk until well amalgamated, light and fluffy.

Using a spoon, fold in the double cream.

Serve with biscuits.

Ricotta pudding with pear

1 pear, peeled, cored and cut into small cubes

100ml/3½fl oz water

25g/1oz sugar

1 teaspoon lemon juice

1 quantity ricotta pudding

Put the pear, water, sugar and lemon juice in a small pan and place on a low heat. Cook until the pear softens but is not mushy.

Leave to cool and stir into the basic ricotta mixture.

Ricotta pudding with cinnamon and dried fruits

pinch of powdered cinnamon

zest of ½ orange

50g/1¾oz candied fruits

1 quantity ricotta pudding

Stir the cinnamon, orange and candied fruits into the basic ricotta pudding.

Ricotta pudding with chocolate chips

30g/1oz pistachio nuts, roughly chopped

25g/1oz chocolate chips

1 quantity ricotta pudding

Stir the pistachios and chocolate into the basic ricotta pudding.

Cakes
& Biscuits

Even though we have a vast array of ready-made cakes and biscuits on the market today, there is nothing nicer than the smell of baking, or being presented with a homemade cake for your birthday. It may not be so even, and the biscuits may be misshapen, but the taste will always beat the over-sweet, mass-produced, shop-bought ones. Some people are nervous of baking, but a simple sponge takes only minutes to prepare, especially with an electric whisk. And most biscuits are really simple, too, and they often take even less time to cook. There is nothing more magical than baking a cake or cookies or whatever else takes your fancy.

I don't have much time to cook cakes and make biscuits at home these days but, ever since the girls were toddlers, Liz has tried to involve them in home baking. They love adding the ingredients, mixing them together, and watching the cake grow and the biscuits expand in the oven. The excitement on their faces when it is time to take out whatever treat has been baking, is such a joy to see. It takes me back to when I was a child and would help or watch my mother and sisters bake. I think it is such a wonderful tradition to pass down.

La torta di banane di Olivia
Olivia's banana cake

150g/5½oz butter, softened, plus extra for greasing

100g/3½oz light soft brown sugar

2 eggs, beaten

2 large ripe bananas, peeled and mashed

50g/1¾oz sultanas

50g/1¾oz walnuts, roughly chopped

150g/5½oz self-raising flour, sifted

This recipe is my daughter Olivia's. She was off school one day recovering from chickenpox when she begged Liz to make a banana cake. Olivia was so determined that she got out all the ingredients, so Liz really did not have much choice! Olivia helped to grease the tin, mash the bananas and mix it together. As soon as the cake was out of the oven she helped herself to two giant slices! The cake was a success and we all enjoyed what was left of it. The bananas make the cake wonderfully moist and, if you prefer, you can replace the walnuts with pumpkin seeds or other nuts such as flaked almonds or ground hazelnuts. The sultanas can be replaced by raisins, currants or any other chopped dried fruit.

Pre-heat the oven to 180°C/350°F/Gas 4. Grease and line a 20 × 9cm/ 8 × 3½in loaf tin with baking paper.

Beat the butter and sugar until light and fluffy. Gradually whisk in the beaten eggs. If you notice the mixture begins to curdle, quickly add a couple of tablespoons of the flour.

Add the mashed bananas, sultanas and walnuts. Gently fold in the flour until all the ingredients are well amalgamated.

Pour the mixture into the prepared loaf tin and bake in the oven for about 35 minutes until golden.

Remove, leave to cool, remove from the tin, peel off the baking paper and serve, or place in an airtight container.

Cantucci al cioccolato
Chocolate and hazelnut biscuits

125g/4½oz butter, at room temperature, plus extra for greasing

200g/7oz sugar

2 eggs, beaten

2 teaspoons vanilla essence

1 tablespoon dark rum

300g/10½oz self-raising flour, plus extra for rolling

75g/2¾oz polenta flour

½ teaspoon salt

75g/2¾oz cocoa powder

200g/7oz whole peeled hazelnuts, toasted

zest of 1 orange

Cantucci are traditional Tuscan biscuits, which are usually used to dip into the dessert wine, vin santo. These are a little different, though, as they contain chocolate as well as hazelnuts. They are equally delicious with a cup of tea or a frothy cappuccino. The recipe is simple to make but when you take them out of the oven the first time, make sure you have a really good and sharp serrated knife to cut through the dough in one hit and work quickly.

Pre-heat the oven to 180°C/350°F/Gas 4. Lightly grease a flat baking tray with butter, then line it with greaseproof paper.

Cream the butter and sugar in a bowl until light and fluffy. Add the beaten eggs, vanilla essence and rum, and beat well.

In another bowl, sift and combine the flours, salt and cocoa. Fold into the butter and sugar mixture, then add the hazelnuts and orange zest and mix well until you obtain a dough-like consistency.

Place the dough on a lightly floured work surface and knead a little – if you find it too sticky, add a little more self-raising flour. Divide into two halves and roll each one into a large sausage shape roughly 5cm/2in wide. Press down on them slightly to make a long oval sausage.

Transfer to the greased baking tray and bake them in the pre-heated oven for about 15–20 minutes until cooked. Check by inserting a skewer in the centre – if it comes out dry, they are ready to come out.

Remove them from the oven and cut each sausage into 1cm/½in slices with a good, sharp serrated knife. Lay them flat on the baking tray and put them back in the oven for a further 10 minutes until crunchy.

Remove, allow to cool, and serve, or store in an airtight container.

Torta all'olio
Olive oil cake

a little butter for greasing

250g/9oz self-raising flour

1 egg

125g/4½oz sugar

125ml/4fl oz milk

4 tablespoons olive oil

grated zest of 1 lemon

2 tablespoons rum

for the berry sauce

200g/7oz mixed berries, either fresh or frozen

½ glass water

juice of 1 orange

50g/1¾oz sugar

Traditionally cakes in Italy were always made with olive oil instead of butter. This was a plain but homely cake and made with ingredients people always had at home. Olive oil cake is still made in certain households today where butter is not used, especially in southern Italy. I have added the recipe for a berry sauce to serve with the cake, if desired. You could leave the berry sauce to harden, slice the cake in half and spread with the sauce as a jam filling. You can, of course, enjoy the cake by itself without making the sauce. It is ideal at teatime and also for breakfast.

Pre-heat the oven to 180°C/350°F/Gas 4. Grease a 20cm/8in round cake tin lightly with butter and dust it with flour.

Place the cake ingredients in a bowl and mix together thoroughly.

Pour into the prepared cake tin and bake in the oven for 30–35 minutes until golden.

Meanwhile, make the sauce by placing all the ingredients in a pan over a medium heat. Simmer for about 10 minutes until it begins to thicken. Remove, leave to rest for a couple of minutes and then serve with the cake, if desired.

Brutti ma buoni
Nutty biscuits

a little butter for greasing

2 egg whites

pinch of salt

120g/4¼oz sugar

55g/2oz almonds, finely chopped

55g/2oz hazelnuts, finely chopped

In northern Italy these traditional biscuits are very common in pastry shops. Brutti ma buoni, literally translated into English, means ugly but good – which will become clear when you make them! They are easy to make and delicious to keep in your biscuit tin for teatime.

Pre-heat the oven to 170°C/325°F/Gas 3 and grease a baking tray with a little bit of butter.

Whisk the egg whites over a bain-marie with a pinch of salt until stiff.

Add the sugar and nuts, and continue to whisk over the bain-marie until the mixture begins to look caramelized. At this stage, remove from the bain-marie.

Place half tablespoons of the mixture on to the prepared baking tray and cook in the oven for 15–20 minutes until set.

Biscotti
Italian cookies

120g/4¼oz plain flour, plus extra for rolling

80g/3oz semolina flour

pinch of salt

50g/1¾oz sugar

120g/4¼oz butter, softened

1 egg

40g/1½oz dark chocolate, finely chopped, or chocolate chips

1 teaspoon rum essence (optional)

soft brown sugar to sprinkle

These are nice little biscuits that are perfect for children. There is very little sugar in them and I used plain chocolate which is not very sweet either but, if you prefer, do use milk chocolate. When I made them to test the recipe for this book, they disappeared in seconds – my girls just loved them!

Pre-heat the oven to 180°C/350°F/Gas 4.

On a clean work surface, combine the flours, salt, sugar, butter, egg, chocolate and rum essence, if using. Mix well with your hands until you obtain a smooth pastry.

Sprinkle the work surface with flour and roll the pastry out to a thickness of about 3mm/⅛in. Cut into shapes with a 5cm/2in diameter pastry cutter, place on a baking tray and prick each biscuit with a fork.

Sprinkle with some soft brown sugar and bake in the oven for about 15–20 minutes until golden.

Remove, leave to cool a little and serve, or store in an airtight container.

Savoiardi
Sponge fingers

a little butter for greasing

3 eggs, separated

120g/4¼oz sugar

70g/2½oz plain flour, sifted

20g/¾oz potato flour, sifted

pinch of salt

a couple of drops of lemon juice

20g/¾oz icing sugar, sifted

The classic Italian Savoiardi biscuits are widely used in Italian desserts, such as tiramisu, but are also lovely to eat on their own. They are light and easy to digest and are given to babies in Italy. Although they are available in shops, it is nice to make your own. They are quick and easy to make, and can be stored in an airtight container to use when required.

Pre-heat the oven to 200°C/400°F/Gas 6. Grease a baking tray with a little butter and line with baking paper.

In a bowl, beat the egg yolks and 50g/1¾oz of the sugar until light and fluffy. Set aside.

In another bowl, whisk the egg whites and 50g/1¾oz of the sugar until stiff.

Fold the flours and salt gently into the egg yolk mixture. Add the lemon juice and carefully fold the stiffened egg whites into this mixture.

Place the mixture in a piping bag with a smooth nozzle and pipe 6cm/2½in fingers on to the prepared baking tray. Make sure you have space between each biscuit as they will expand during baking.

Combine the icing sugar with the remaining 20g/¾oz of sugar and sprinkle this over each finger. Place in the oven for 15 minutes until golden.

Remove, allow to cool, then gently remove from the baking paper. Serve or store in an airtight container.

Tip: If you pipe the mixture into rounds, once cooked and cooled, slice and fill with some jam or chocolate spread to make a biscuit sandwich!

Dolce d'amalfi
Lemon and almond cake

130g/4½oz butter, soft, plus extra for greasing

160g/5¾ oz icing sugar

grated zest of 2 unwaxed good-quality lemons, plus extra for garnishing

60g/2¼oz candied lemon peel, finely chopped

pinch of salt

1 vanilla pod

2 eggs, at room temperature

80g/3oz plain flour

5g/⅛oz baking powder

50g/1¾oz potato starch

100g/3½oz ground almonds

100ml/3½fl oz milk, at room temperature

2 lemon slices, some lemon zest and 1 lemon leaf (optional)

This comes from Salvatore De Riso, a pastry chef from my home town in Italy. He and his family own Pasticcieria De Riso in Minori, which makes the best cakes ever! I can't wait for my next visit to enjoy more delicious treats. This cake is wonderfully light and moist with a delicate taste of lemon and almonds. When I make it the smells transport me back home.

Pre-heat the oven to 180°C/350°F/Gas 4. Grease a 20cm/8in diameter round cake tin with a little butter, and line with baking paper.

Cream the icing sugar and butter together. Add the lemon zest, candied peel, salt and vanilla pod. Stir in the eggs, one at a time. Sift the flour, baking powder and potato starch into the mixture and combine. Stir in the ground almonds. Gradually add the milk and stir well.

Remove the vanilla pod, pour the mixture into the prepared baking tin and bake for 40 minutes.

Once it is ready, remove from the oven and leave to cool before garnishing with lemon slices, zest and leaf, if desired and serving.

Ciambella
Traditional ring cake

300g/10½oz butter, plus extra for greasing

300g/10½oz sugar

pinch of salt

6 eggs, beaten

2 teaspoons grated orange zest, plus extra for decorating (optional)

150g/5½oz good-quality milk chocolate, melted and cooled, plus extra chocolate curls to decorate (optional)

300g/10½oz self-raising flour, sifted

This is a traditional Italian cake baked in a ring tin. It has been made by housewives throughout Italy for centuries, adding different ingredients depending on the desired flavour. In this particular recipe, the combination of chocolate and orange is delicious.

Pre-heat the oven to 170°C/325°F/Gas 3. Grease a 28cm/11in ring tin with butter and dust with flour.

Cream the butter, sugar and pinch of salt until light and fluffy.

Add the beaten eggs gradually until well amalgamated – if you notice the mixture begins to curdle, quickly add a couple of tablespoons of the flour. Stir in the orange zest.

Divide the mixture, pouring half into another bowl.

In one bowl, fold in the melted chocolate and half of the flour. In the other, fold in the remaining flour.

Pour the chocolate mixture into the ring tin, and then pour the plain mixture on top.

Bake in the pre-heated oven for about 45 minutes. Test with a skewer – if it comes out dry, the cake is cooked.

Remove from the oven, allow to cool a little, decorated with orange zest and chocolate curls, if using, and then serve, or store in an airtight tin.

Tip: If you notice the top of the cake getting too brown while it is cooking, cover with a sheet of greaseproof paper.

Leftovers

Using leftover food to make quick, delicious and healthy meals for the following day makes so much sense. In fact, it is almost worth making extra, in order to have a speedy meal for the next day's lunch or dinner.

Leftover risotto can make wonderful dishes, such as Arancini (see page 230) or, by adding some Tomato or Basic White Sauce (see pages 164 and 173) and cooking in the oven, you can have a fantastic baked risotto – serve both with a simple salad to make a quick and nutritious meal.

Leftover pasta – fried, baked or turned into a salad – is really delicious, too. For a frittata, you just need to beat some eggs, add any leftover vegetables, cheese or ham, and mix well with the leftover pasta. Then, heat some extra virgin olive oil in a frying pan, pour in the mixture and cook as you would an omelette, not forgetting to ensure a crust is formed (see page 231). If you want to bake it, add Tomato Sauce (see page 164) and/or Basic White Sauce (see page 173) and, of course, lots of cheese, and put it in the oven until hot through and bubbling. If you don't have the time or inclination to make fresh sauces, simply add some cheese and butter to the pasta and then bake for about 20 minutes. And, served cold, leftover pasta is a filling and delicious addition to any salad.

I never throw away leftover vegetables either. These can be made into a cheesy vegetable bake or they can be heated through in a frying pan with some extra virgin olive oil, garlic and chilli, to liven them up the next day. They can even be added to pasta or risotto dishes.

Leftover roast chicken or other kinds of poultry can make wonderful salads (see page 232). Leftover roast beef can be minced to make yummy burgers or meat balls, or it can simply be sliced and served cold.

I remember when I was growing up, our family never threw out any leftover food; it was either reheated the next day or made into a whole new dish for all the family to enjoy. Sometimes dishes like the Ciambotta di Verdure (see page 126) can taste even nicer the next day. The flavours infuse and the taste is more intense. This is true of soups and stews, and my mother often made extra on purpose. We would have a wonderful meal to enjoy the following day, without her having to cook again. We didn't have a freezer in those days, so we could not keep things for longer than that, but now it's worth making even more because soups and stews are so easy to freeze. (Please refer to your freezer manual to check how long you can keep homemade food in the freezer, and always label your containers with the name of the dish and the date of making.) Freezing freshly home-cooked food really does make life simpler, especially for working parents or even for people who live on their own but don't want to eat ready-made, processed food and takeaways.

There is such a variety of delicious dishes that can be made with leftovers and there are a handful of recipes which I hope you find useful. But I leave it to you to think of more ways to cook leftovers – use your imagination and I'm sure you will come up with lots of different and interesting recipes. In fact, I bet you could write a whole book! Be proud of not being wasteful, and also be proud of the many new dishes you create.

Arancini
Fried risotto balls

375g/13oz leftover risotto

plain flour for dusting

2 eggs, beaten

300g/10½oz breadcrumbs for coating

oil for frying

These make a lovely snack or starter when you have leftover risotto. I have not specified the kind of risotto you'll need because any flavour will do – even a plain version, as in the recipe on page 76. You can fill the risotto balls with extra leftovers, too, such as mozzarella, ham, peas or Bolognese sauce, and this makes them lovely and moist. Otherwise, just make them as described below: they are truly delicious!

Take a little of the leftover risotto at a time and form into balls roughly the size of a golf ball. (If you want to fill them, make an indentation and press your filling inside. Reshape the ball so the filling is in the centre and completely covered by the risotto.)

Dust the risotto balls with flour, then coat in the beaten eggs, followed by the breadcrumbs.

Heat some oil in a large deep saucepan or a deep-fat fryer. When the oil is hot enough, add the risotto balls a few at a time. Fry for 2–3 minutes until golden. Remove with a slotted spoon and drain on kitchen paper.

Serve hot or cold.

Tip: If you don't have the right amount of risotto, just use what you have and adjust the quantities of egg and breadcrumbs accordingly. To test whether the oil is hot enough, drop in a small piece of bread – if it sizzles and browns it is ready.

Frittata di spaghetti farcita
Filled spaghetti omelette

3 eggs

100g/3½oz Parmesan cheese

350g/12oz leftover cooked spaghetti

80g/3oz butter, melted

8 basil leaves, roughly torn

3 tablespoons extra virgin olive oil

4 tablespoons leftover tomato sauce or 8 cherry tomatoes, sliced in half

60g/2¼oz hard mozzarella or other leftover cheese

salt and pepper

A great way of using up leftover cooked spaghetti, tagliatelle or any other long pasta shape. The filling gives the dish a fresh taste and no one need know you are using leftover pasta! Serve with a simple green salad.

Beat the eggs in a bowl and then add the Parmesan and season with salt and pepper. Stir in the cooked spaghetti and pour in the melted butter. Add the basil and mix well.

Heat the olive oil in a non-stick frying pan over a medium heat. Pour in half of the omelette mixture and even out with a fork. Cook for a minute.

Place either the tomato sauce or cherry tomatoes on top, followed by the mozzarella. Pour over the remaining omelette mixture. Cook for 5–8 minutes, until a crust is formed on the bottom, then carefully flip over and continue to cook on the other side until it turns golden brown.

Remove and serve immediately or eat cold.

Insalata di pollo, ricotta e pasta
Chicken salad with ricotta and pasta topped with crunchy bacon

300g/10½oz fusilli pasta, cooked until *al dente* and left to cool

150g/5½oz cooked chicken, roughly chopped

100g/3½oz baby spinach leaves

150g/5½oz ricotta

4 tablespoons extra virgin olive oil

4 slices bacon, grilled until very crispy and roughly chopped

salt and pepper

A really simple recipe using leftover boiled or roasted chicken.

Place the pasta, chicken and baby spinach leaves in a serving dish.

In a small bowl, mix the ricotta with 2 tablespoons of the olive oil and season with salt and pepper.

Add the ricotta dressing to the pasta and chicken and mix well, making sure everything is well coated. Top with the crispy bacon, drizzle with the remaining olive oil and serve.

Tip: If you find you have some of this left over, place it in an ovenproof dish with some fontina cheese over the top and cook in a hot oven for about 15 minutes to make a lovely baked pasta dish.

Polpettine di pane
Bread dumplings

80g/3oz butter

30g/1oz onion, finely chopped

100g/3½oz pancetta or bacon, finely chopped

350g/12oz stale bread, crusts removed and cut into cubes

200ml/7fl oz milk

1 tablespoon parsley, finely chopped

pinch of grated nutmeg

1 egg, beaten

50g/1¾oz plain flour, plus extra for dusting your hands

1.5 litres/2¾ pints stock or Beef Broth (see page 41)

20g/¾oz Parmesan cheese, freshly grated

salt and pepper

This is a great way of using up leftover bread and makes a most nutritious meal. You can either serve these dumplings in the broth they are cooked in as a soup, or drain them and serve with a simple Tomato Sauce (see page 164) or a Butter Sauce (see page 163). Although a much-loved Northern Italian/Germanic recipe, it is a popular way of using up bread throughout Italy.

Heat the butter in a pan over a medium heat and sweat the onion. Stir in the pancetta or bacon and bread, and cook until crunchy.

Remove from the heat, stir in the milk and leave to soften.

Add the parsley, nutmeg, egg and plain flour, and season with salt and pepper. Mix well to amalgamate.

Flour your hands and form the mixture into balls roughly the size of a walnut. Set aside.

Heat the stock or Beef Broth in a saucepan. At boiling point, drop in the dumplings. When they float back up to the surface, continue to cook for a further 7 minutes.

Serve a few dumplings per person with the broth, or coated in a sauce of your choice. Sprinkle with grated Parmesan.

Insalata di trota, patate e broccoli
Trout salad with potatoes and broccoli

500g/1lb 2oz baby new potatoes

1 broccoli head, cut into florets

90ml/6 tablespoons extra virgin olive oil

½ tablespoon finely chopped dill

½ tablespoon finely chopped chives

300g/10½oz cooked fillet of trout, cut into chunks

2 shallots, finely sliced

salt and pepper

An easy-to-prepare salad that makes use of leftover cooked trout, or any other fish, and can even be made with leftover potatoes and broccoli. The combination of ingredients is a perfect and nutritionally balanced meal.

Place the potatoes in a pan of water over a medium heat and boil until tender. Drain and cool.

Cook the broccoli in a pan of boiling water for just a few minutes until tender but still crunchy. Drain and place the broccoli in iced water to keep it fresh and shiny while assembling the salad.

Mix the olive oil, dill and chives, and season with salt and pepper. Whisk with a fork until well amalgamated and creamy.

In a large bowl combine the trout, potatoes, broccoli and shallots, and pour over the dressing, mixing well. Leave to rest for a couple of minutes, then serve.

Sandwich di mozzarella dorata
Cooked mozzarella sandwich

180g/6¼oz courgettes

2 tablespoons extra virgin olive oil

1 garlic clove, whole

1 tablespoon parsley, finely chopped

4 eggs

25g/1oz butter, softened

2 tablespoons milk

2 tablespoons Parmesan cheese, grated

4 cherry tomatoes, finely chopped

400g/14oz block of hard mozzarella, cut lengthways into 4 slices, then each slice cut in half (you should aim for 8 roughly square slices of mozzarella about 3 or 4mm/⅛ or ¼in thick)

plain flour for dusting

400g/14oz breadcrumbs

oil for frying

salt and pepper

A good way of using up leftover hard mozzarella, though it's not just a straightforward mozzarella sandwich as the title suggests. There are a few stages to this recipe, but it is simple and worth making as it is really delicious. If you prefer, you can replace the courgettes with aubergines. This makes a nourishing snack or meal, when served with a fresh tomato or green salad.

Slice the courgettes into thin strips, then cut into small cubes and set aside.

Heat the olive oil in a pan, add the garlic and sweat over a medium heat. Discard the garlic and stir in the courgette cubes. Season with salt and pepper and stir-fry until soft. Remove from the heat, stir in the parsley and leave to cool.

In a bowl beat two of the eggs together with the butter and milk, and season with salt and pepper. Stir in the Parmesan and pour into a pan over a medium heat. Scramble until the eggs reach a solid consistency. Pour away the excess liquid.

Drain the cooled, fried courgettes of excess oil and fold into the scrambled egg mixture, along with the cherry tomatoes.

Dust the mozzarella slices in plain flour and spread the eggy mixture on to 4 of the slices, ensuring the filling does not go to the edges. Top each of these slices with another slice of mozzarella, pressing the edges together well so the filling does not escape.

Beat the remaining two eggs (you may find you need more). Coat each mozzarella sandwich in the beaten eggs, then in the breadcrumbs. Repeat the procedure – the egg and breadcrumb coating is done twice to make the end result really crispy and golden.

Heat the frying oil in a large pan over a high heat. When hot, fry each sandwich for about 1 minute on each side.

Remove and drain on kitchen paper and serve. These are delicious eaten hot but can also be served cold, if desired.

Insalata di carne lessa all'arancia
Cold beef salad with orange

800g/1lb 12oz cooked beef

15 pitted green olives, halved or quartered

1 fennel, thinly sliced

6 cherry tomatoes, roughly chopped

1 orange, peel and pith removed, separated into segments

300g/10½oz mixed salad

for the dressing

zest and juice of ½ orange

1 tablespoon lemon juice

90ml/6 tablespoons extra virgin olive oil

hairy fronds from the fennel, finely chopped

salt and pepper

This recipe is a good way of using up the boiled beef from the Beef Broth recipe (see page 41). You could have the broth with some pastina one evening and this salad the next day. Quick and simple to prepare, it's great for when you're in a hurry.

Roughly chop the beef, combine with the olives, fennel, tomatoes, orange segments and salad.

Combine all the dressing ingredients and whisk well. Pour over the beef salad and serve.

Arrosti misti
Mixed roasts

a selection of leftover meats: chicken pieces (e.g. quarters, drumsticks, breasts); rack of lamb or lamb cutlets; pork fillet or cutlets; piece of beef, cut into chunks

1kg/2lb 4oz potatoes, peeled and chopped into thick segments

90ml/6 tablespoons extra virgin olive oil

needles of 1 rosemary branch

3 sage leaves

1 garlic clove

a few slices of pancetta or bacon, if using leftover pork

salt and pepper

for the marinade

3 garlic cloves

2 onions, finely chopped

needles of 2 rosemary branches

a few sage leaves

2 thyme branches

2 bay leaves

6 peppercorns

200ml/7fl oz white wine

Quite often I find I have small quantities of different types of meat that are not enough by themselves to make a meal. So I put them together with lots of herbs to make a lovely roast. I find the meat is tastier and gives off a wonderful herby aroma if you marinate it. Once marinated, it is really quick and simple to cook. I have not given quantities for the meat as this depends on what you have, but the marinade ingredients are roughly enough for 4 servings of meat. Please note this recipe is for small pieces of meat – large pieces will need more time in the oven.

Pre-heat the oven to 200°C/400°F/Gas 6.

First prepare the marinade by combining all the ingredients. Pour this over the pieces of meat and leave to marinate while you prepare the rest of the dish.

Place the potatoes in a bowl with a drizzle of the olive oil, the rosemary, sage and garlic, and season with salt and pepper. Set aside.

Heat the remaining olive oil in a roasting tin large enough to accommodate all the meat and potatoes. Add the garlic, onion and herbs from the marinade and sweat over a medium heat. Add the pieces of meat and seal well on all sides. Add the juices from the marinade and allow to evaporate. Season with salt and pepper.

Remove from the heat, wrap bacon slices around the pork, scatter the potatoes around the meats, cover with foil and put in the oven for 20 minutes.

Take off the foil and continue to roast for a further 15 minutes, until all the cuts of meat are cooked.

Remove from the oven, leave to rest for a couple of minutes and serve.

Cioccolatini di frutta secca
Fruit and nut chocolate treats

130g/4½oz dark or milk chocolate

100g/3½oz toasted whole hazelnuts or walnuts

50g/1¾oz mixed dried fruit (e.g. currants, sultanas, raisins and pine kernels)

20g/¾oz candied fruit

1 tablespoon rum (optional)

redcurrants, coloured sprinkles, stars or silver balls to decorate

8 fairy cake paper cases

Made with leftovers, these delicious little treats are ideal for the Christmas period, or just after, when your cupboard is full of all those half packets of sultanas, currants, raisins, candied fruit and nuts, and even chocolate. I have suggested making eight in the standard-sized paper cases, but if you make them smaller and pack them into a nice box, they'd make a lovely present.

Melt 80g/3oz of the chocolate in a heatproof bowl over a saucepan containing a couple of inches of barely simmering water.

Remove from the heat and add the nuts, dried and candied fruits, and rum. Mix well.

Leave to rest for a minute, then put dollops of the mixture into the paper cases. Leave to cool completely.

Melt the remaining chocolate and use a spoon to drizzle it over the cooled treats.

Decorate as you like, leave to set and serve.

Tip: These treats can be stored in an airtight tin for at least a week.

Crema e pandoro
Toasted pandoro slices with Italian custard cream

6 egg yolks

80g/3oz sugar

500ml/18fl oz hot milk

55g/2 oz plain flour

1 teaspoon of vanilla essence or the seeds from 1 vanilla pod

2 large slices of pandoro, cut into triangles

sifted icing sugar to sprinkle

This is a good way of using up leftover pandoro, the Italian Christmas cake, which comes from the Veneto region. Pandoro is often preferred to panettone because of its light vanilla taste and the absence of dried and candied fruit, and it is now becoming popular in this country. Both, of course, are equally good in my opinion!

Whisk the egg yolks and sugar. Add a tablespoon of the hot milk and continue to whisk. When light and creamy, whisk in the flour. Add the rest of the hot milk and continue to whisk.

Pour the mixture into a pan and place over a medium heat, stirring all the time with a wooden spoon. Cook until the mixture begins to thicken, then remove from the heat, stir in the vanilla, and leave to cool.

Sprinkle the pandoro triangles with some icing sugar on both sides and place under a hot grill to toast, turning once.

Spoon the cooled custard cream into 4 bowls and arrange the toasted pandoro slices over the top. Serve immediately.

Tip: If you prefer, you can work quickly to serve both the custard cream and pandoro triangles warm. You could also flavour the custard with orange zest and/or orange liqueur, with lemon zest and/or some limoncello, or even give it an aniseed flavour by adding Sambuca and candied fruits.

Other ways of using up leftover pandoro: Use pandoro slices instead of sponge finger biscuits to make Tiramisu (see page 195); cut out shapes from pandoro slices with pastry cutters and fill with jam, cream or nutella to make sweet sandwiches; toast pandoro slices and enjoy with jam for breakfast or at tea time.

Salame di cioccolato
Chocolate salami

2 egg yolks

100g/3½oz sugar

100g/3½oz dark chocolate, roughly chopped

100g/3½oz butter, at room temperature

200g/7oz plain biscuits, crushed

200g/7oz dried tropical fruit mix, roughly chopped, or a selection of dried pineapple, pear, cranberries, apricots and ginger

50g/1¾oz cocoa

2 sheets of greaseproof paper and cling film

Tip: After slicing, you could pipe double cream or mascarpone on to each slice and top with a piece of fruit to make a sweet canapé. A rich but lovely dessert!

This recipe has been around for quite a few years in Italian kitchens as a way of using up bits of leftover biscuit, dried fruit and chocolate. Years ago, Italy didn't have the wide variety of tropical dried fruits it does now and they would have used whatever was in the cupboard, such as raisins, sultanas, pine kernels, candied peel, prunes and nuts. I find using tropical fruits gives a fresher, original flavour to this recipe. You could also add liqueur, though I haven't as I make it for the children. Simple and with no baking involved, these chocolate salamis are a nutritious biscuit dessert.

Beat the egg yolks and sugar until creamy and fluffy.

Melt the chocolate with the butter in a heatproof bowl over a saucepan containing a couple of inches of barely simmering water. Remove from the heat and gradually add the beaten egg yolk mixture.

Stir in the biscuits, dried fruit and 30g of the cocoa. Mix all together until well amalgamated. Divide into two.

Take the sheets of greaseproof paper and wet them under a cold-running tap. Squeeze with your hands to remove the excess liquid and open them out flat on a work surface. Place one half of the chocolate mixture in the centre of each sheet. With the help of the greaseproof paper, roll them into sausage shapes about 20cm/8in. Roll them up tightly in the paper, securing at the ends like a cracker. Then wrap them in cling film. Put both in the freezer for 20 minutes to harden.

Remove from the freezer, take off the cling film and put in the fridge for 15 minutes.

Remove from fridge, unroll from the paper, sift the remaining cocoa powder over the top, cut the salami into slices and place on a serving dish. Put any leftovers back in the fridge until required.

index

Note: Vegetarian recipes include eggs and dairy products, and are indicated in the general index by a bracketed 'v'. To save space, English recipe titles only are given in subheadings.